*For my son Christopher.*

My thanks to everyone who has contributed to this book:

To all the illustrators who generously shared their experiences, insights and images:
Shirley Hughes, Pam Smy, Alexis Deacon, Angela Barrett, Marta Altés,
Ashley Crowley, David Hughes, Elena Arevalo, Daisy Hirst, Paula Metcalfe.

Also a big 'thank you' to all the lovely people at Random House,
the Imperial War Museum, Laura Cecil Literary Agency, Walker books, HarperCollins,
Templar Publishing, and Penguin who have granted permission to use their images.

...and to my mum who patiently typed up my manuscript!

Observation

*noun*

1 the action or process of observing something or someone carefully or in order to gain information:
*she was brought into the hospital for observation*
*detailed observations were carried out on the students' behaviour*
the ability to notice things, especially significant details:
*his powers of observation*
the taking of the altitude of the sun or another celestial body for navigational purposes.
2 a remark, statement or comment based on something one has seen, heard, or noticed:
*he made a telling observation about Hugh*

Oxford Dictionary 2012

*From my sketchbook, 'The Mouseboat'*

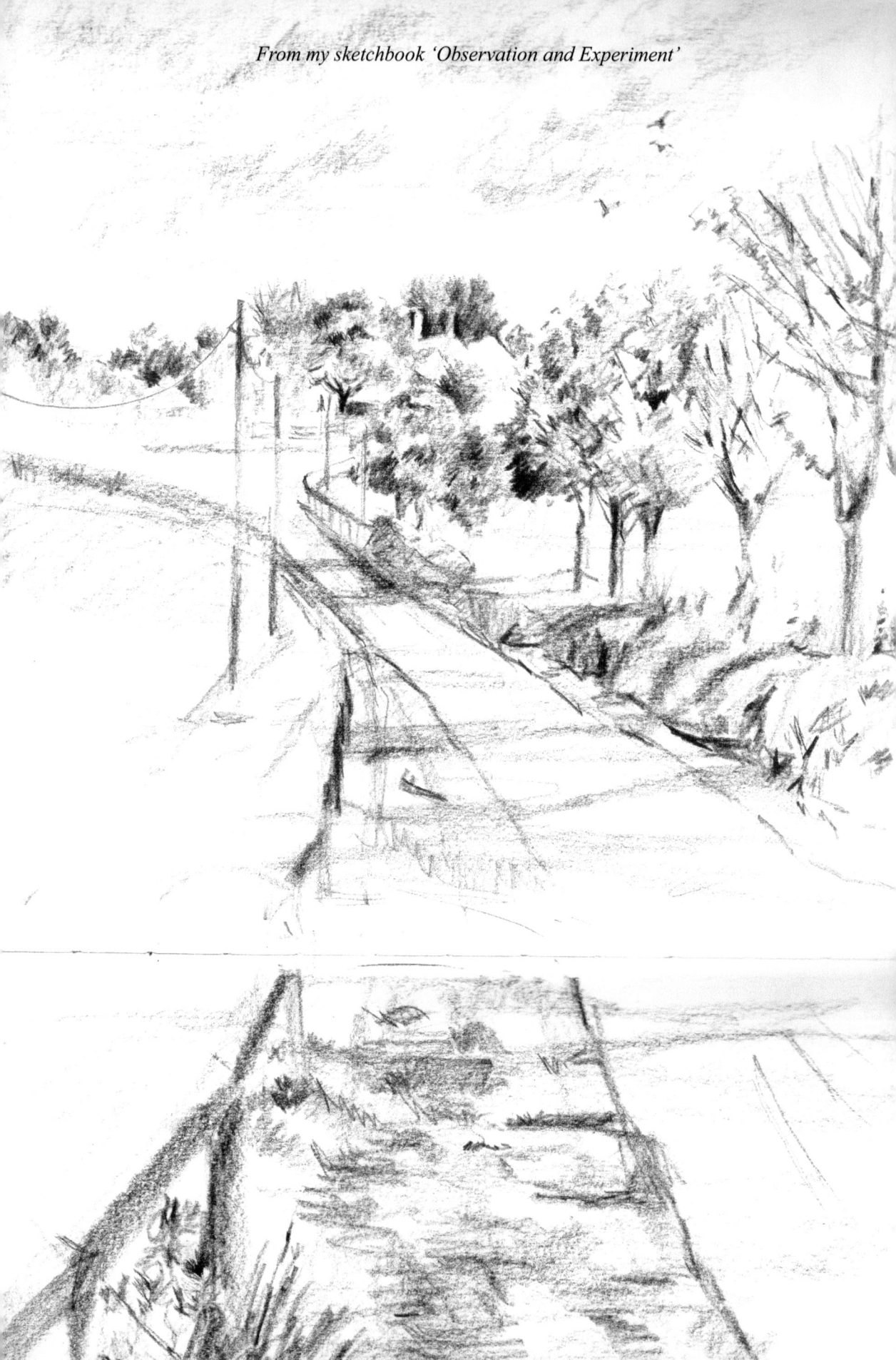

*From my sketchbook 'Observation and Experiment'*

# Contents

3 Introduction

5 Observation and the Development of Visual Communication

15 Observation and the Creation of the Children's Book Narrative

23 Observation and Narrative Non-fiction

33 Observation Leading to Informed Imagination

41 Conclusion

45 References

49 Bibliography

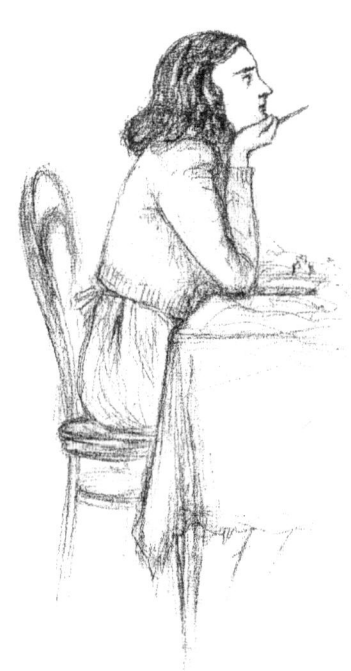

*From Anne Frank by Josephine Poole  published by Hutchinson 2005.*
*Illustration © Angela Barrett, 2005.*
*Reproduced by permission of The Random House Group Ltd.*

*From my sketchbook 'Observation and Experiment'*

# Introduction

Whilst the creation of books for children might appear to be routed in the imaginary, this study investigates the role that observation plays throughout the creative process.

Observation in the context of illustration is often taken to mean drawing from life but the study explores the synthesis of observation which filters throughout the making of stories for children from first concept to the finished outcome of both words and pictures.

My own interest in the role of observation developed alongside my studies on the Children's Book Illustration MA at Cambridge School of Art. As the process of observational drawing developed my own visual language I also wondered at the sometimes miraculous drawing progression of other students.

For the illustrator, learning to draw is not about acquiring the ability to recreate a technically accurate image (for me often resulting in bland outcomes). What we are seeking to acquire is a communication skill capable of transcending reality and transporting an audience to another world.

Alongside the development of communication through drawing, the ability to create compelling narratives also improved; I am sure this is no coincidence.

Joining the course and eager to make illustrations, the general feeling on reading the first assignment entitled '*Observation and Experiment*' was one of slight disappointment and anticlimax, leaving us questioning what this had to do with the business of illustrating for children. Little did we know what an influence the discipline of observation would have on our future practice. These naïve expectations were partly as a result of our familiarity with the stylised imagery of illustrators such as Paula Metcalfe, Oliver Jeffers and Lauren Childs, where visual outcomes, often far removed from real life, lead one to question the place for observation.

This study explores this perceived contradiction and investigates whether observation does play a crucial role in the creative process, even in areas where its importance may not be obvious.

Via the exploration of the practice of children's story makers (both authors and illustrators), the role observation has to play in the creative process is considered.

This valuable analysis and reflection leads to an enriched and informed approach to making books.

*From my sketchbook 'Nepalese Rhino', Whipsnade*

# Observation and the Development of Visual Communication

Walt Disney artist Bernard Garbutt placed the role of observational drawing into context when talking about the practice of drawing animals:

*The idea behind sketching animals is not to produce a collection of animal drawings, but to produce better draftsmen, to broaden the student's scope beyond the human figure. If a student has really observed the structure of an animal when it's standing, he should be able to draw it in other positions as well. The ability to draw animals quickly and convincingly must be acquired through making hundreds of sketches – and thinking about them when you're not sketching.'*

I consider myself very lucky to have discovered drawing and even luckier to have finally learned about the relationship between what I see and the marks I make on the paper. Children's author illustrator Shirley Hughes likens this process of creating images to '*The nearest thing I know to flying into the sun*'. However, often, the biggest frustration for any aspiring illustrator is having wonderful ideas but lacking the tools to recreate them. For an illustrator, learning to draw through observation is about acquiring the drawing confidence and experience to release creativity and realise one's thoughts through pictures.

In an article for '*Famous Artists Magazine*' the American illustrator Al Dorne wrote:

*'To me, drawing is the most important consideration in making pictures. Unless you know how to draw, you won't know the security of being able to express yourself clearly and fluently as an artist....It is also the art of observation and communication.'*

Although I never stopped observing everything around me, the process of illustrating for educational publications, (where the brief is often tightly prescribed and controlled by the editor) led to apathy in my drawing habit and the conceit that I could 'do it already'. Joyfully revisiting the practice of observational drawing during my studies, I began to discover the freedom that learning to see can bring.

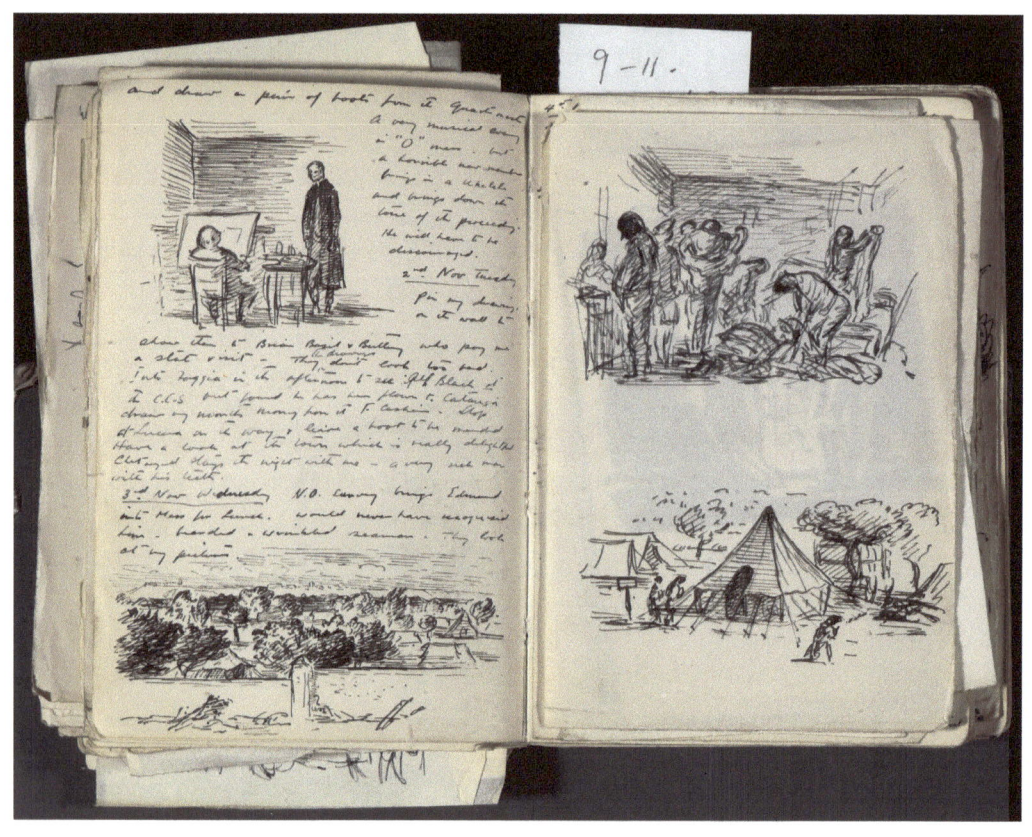

*Diary entries from Diary of a War Artist' © by Edward Ardizzone, Bodley Head 1974*

*Permission granted by the Artist's Estate*
*Scan of original pages courtesy of the Imperial War Museum*
*c/o Laura Cecil Literary Agency (Art.IWM ART LD 7580 a 262b-263a)*

Edward Ardizzone's evocative '*Diary of a War Artist*'[4] suggests that intensive observational study underpinned his work as an illustrator; the ability to capture a moment in simplicity of line is the essence of his children's illustration work. However, Ardizzone would have disagreed. In his talk '*The Born Illustrator*', he commented:

'*There are two things that all born illustrators have in common. The first is that their creative imagination is fired by the written word rather than the thing seen; the second is that when it comes to their illustrations they would rather make them up than have recourse to life.*'[5]

In the same talk, Ardizzone did concede that there was one observational practice that was of value to him as an illustrator:

'*...on looking back, I realise that most of what skill I possess came from that endless doodling at the office, plus copying figures out of the few art books I had at home, Daumier, Rowlandson and Rubens being the favourites. Even now I wish I had paid more attention to this copying. I might have been able to draw better than I do.*'[6]

The aspiring illustrator is of course firmly discouraged from copying the work of others but there is a subliminal observation of the work of other illustrators which filters into our mark making. Copying in the loosest sense could still be construed as observation. Ardizzone adds:

'*A simple example is the making of very black cast shadows to throw up the form, a device which is particularly useful when one is making small drawings of figures in pen and ink. This is a valid trick because it is based on observable fact. It may take a beginner a long time to find it on his own however. Why not pick it up from a master in the art?*'[7]

When one studies the work of other illustrators, observations about technique, medium, depiction of mood and gesture can improve the ability to convey ideas and develop tools for making better pictures.

We don't have to copy to observe.

Observing the work of successful children's illustrators has had an influence on my work from childhood, when I carefully copied the illustrations of Beatrix Potter. This meant I practiced watercolour painting when I was very young and probably why I now find this medium so comforting. On reflection, I can see Potter's influence in the artwork for *'The Mouseboat*₈', although this wasn't a conscious decision. I was keen to ensure that the animals maintained a true-to-life quality (even though they were doing things that don't happen in the natural world).

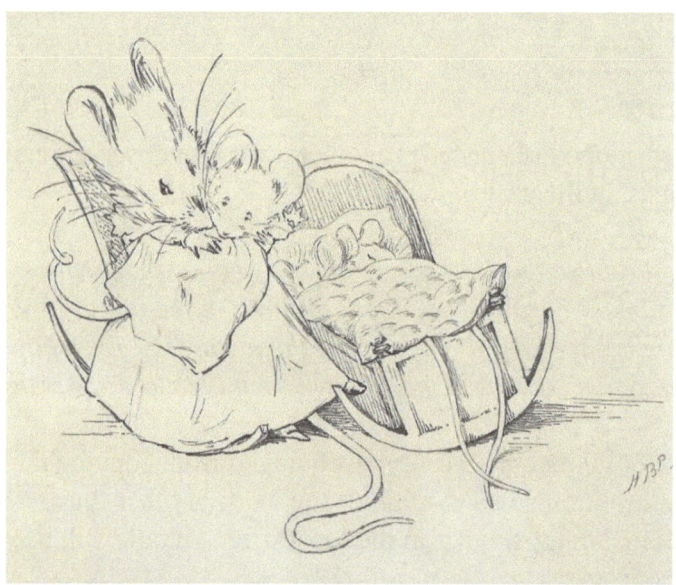

*Original sketch for 'The Tale of Two Bad Mice' by Beatrix Potter, 1904*

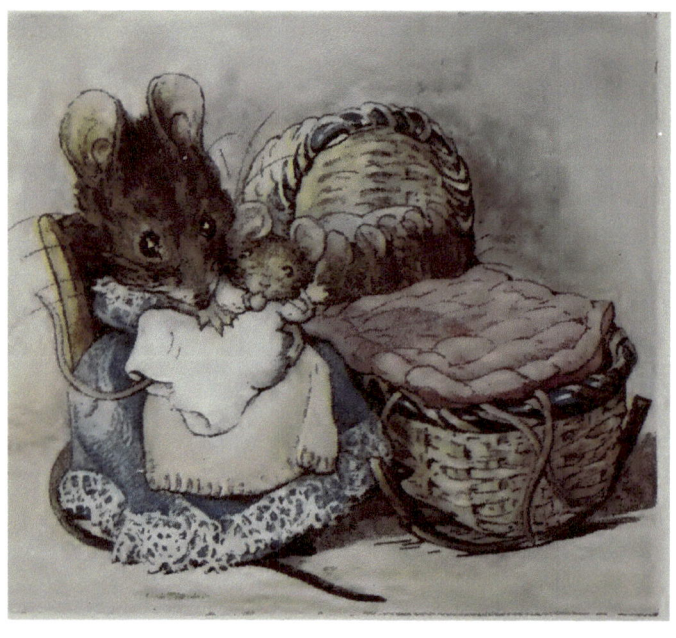

*Illustration from 'The Tale of Two Bad Mice' by Beatrix Potter, 1904*₉

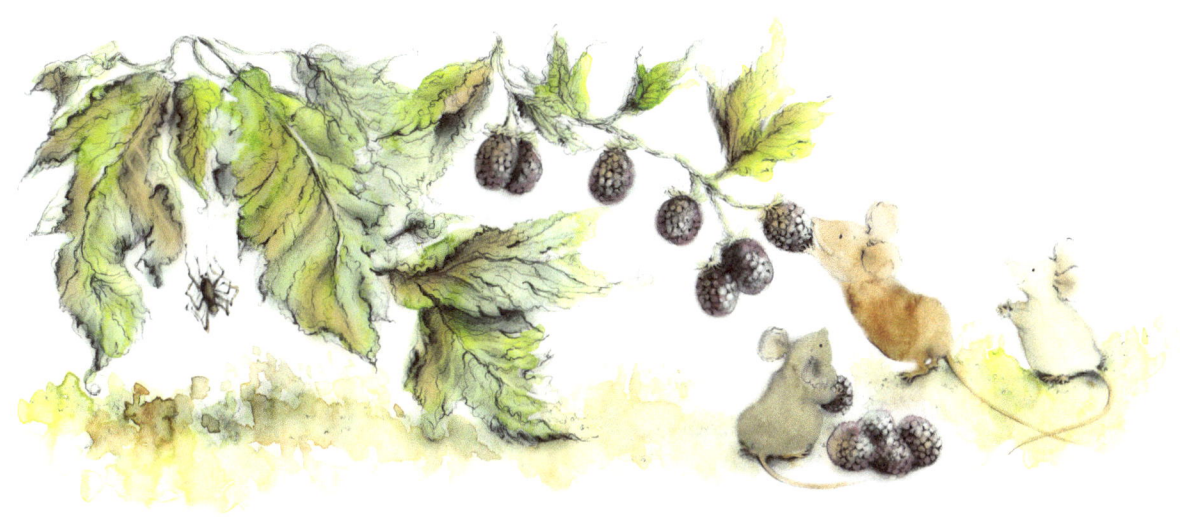

*A spread from my picture book 'The Mouseboat'*[10]

The habit of drawing in a sketchbook everyday builds up a memory bank of imagery. Not only does this provide a huge source of visual reference but the knowledge acquired speeds up the process of getting down what is panning out in your head. Shirley Hughes told me:

*'Observation is vital to me… I carry a sketchbook (not a camera) everywhere. It is an essential memory training, so I can go back to my drawing board and make it all up.'*[11]

I am still trying to get into this habit and 'lack of time' and feeling self conscious are barriers that often get in my way. It is a constant regret and one which I aspire to improve but I am probably never going to be in the habit of the prolific and accomplished 'sketch bookers' such as Shirley Hughes or Pam Smy. I asked the illustrator David Hughes about his use of sketchbooks and was reassured that his lack of time meant he was only now developing their use:

*'For years I didn't use a sketchbook, didn't have time. In the last 10 years or so I will occasionally try out ideas for books and more recently I find myself using them more and I think it's because you are able to scan satisfactory images into the computer and work on them from there.'*[12]

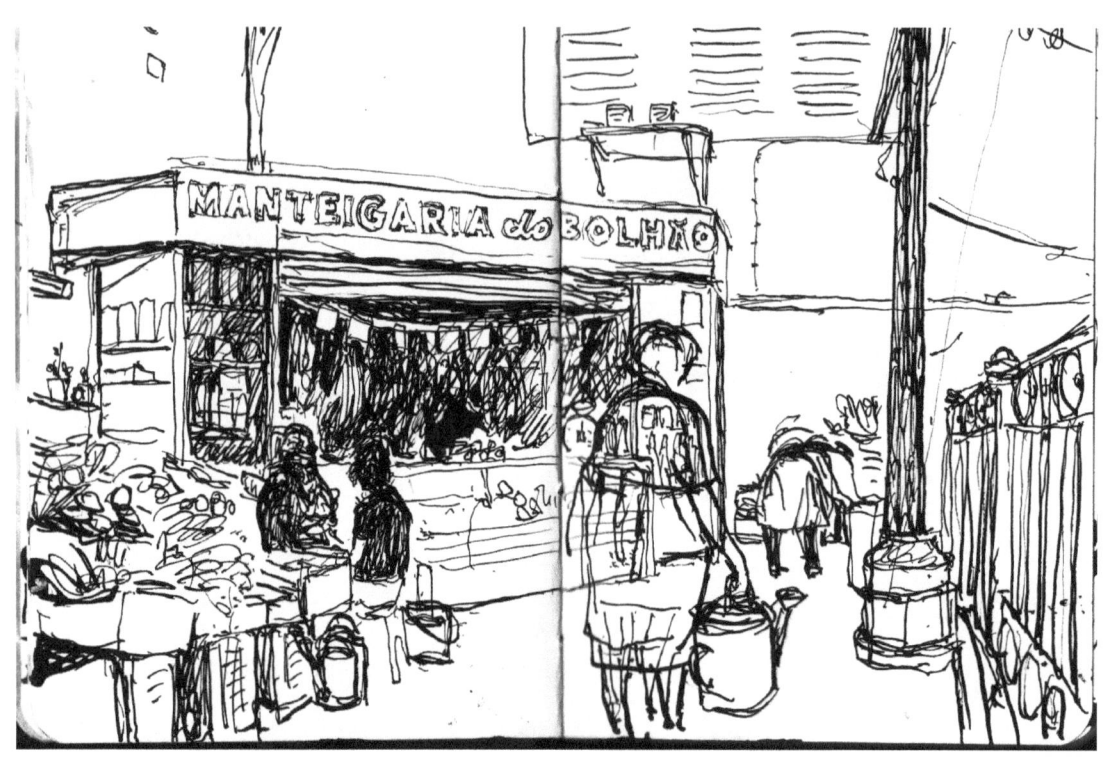

*Sketchbook, Pam Smy, 2012 used with permission.*[13]

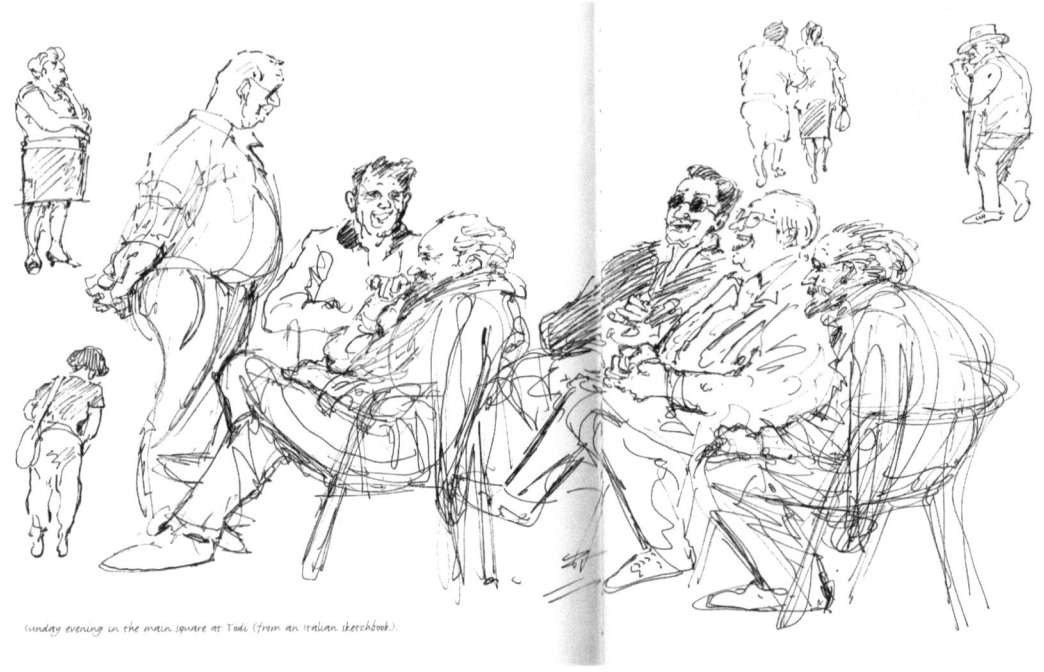

*Sunday evening in the main square at Todi (from an Italian sketchbook).*

*'An Italian Sketchbook', Shirley Hughes*
*From A Life Drawing by Shirley Hughes published by The Bodley Head 2002.*
*Copyright © Shirley Hughes, 2002.* [14]
*Reproduced by permission of The Random House Group Ltd.*

10

When I started working towards *'The Mouseboat'*, I was eager to get on with creating the final illustrations; my idea for the narrative just couldn't wait! But shortcutting my observational preparation resulted in flat and unsatisfactory results.

Disappointed and frustrated, I awoke one morning and realised that only real mice would do. Following a visit to the pet shop the problem was solved with two little mice in a cage in my studio. It was as if drawing became effortless and the mice seamlessly evolved into characters. Observational drawing was taking me to another plain where drawing happens as a result of seeing, rather than as an effort to render.

I was developing my ability to look.

*Characters created before the arrival of the 'real mice'.*

*Observational drawing from my sketchbook 'The Mouseboat'*

Professor, Martin Salisbury believes that observational drawing is an education that greatly benefits all student illustrators:

*'In my experience, those students who have subjected themselves most fully to the often humiliating rigours of observational drawing have, with one or two notable exceptions, been the ones best equipped to go on to successful careers in narrative and sequential illustration.'*[15]

With the increase in my observational drawing practice, I experienced a growing confidence to draw. I have also noticed this with my fellow students, whose best work in my opinion often evolved from their observed sketchbook work. We became observers and now in that habit, see everything and everyone around us as good material for children's books.

Observation has built a foundation for better outcomes.

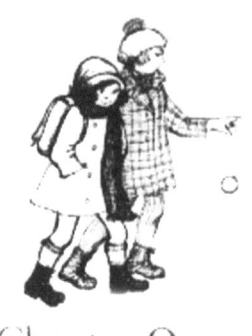

## Chapter One

Anna was walking home from school with Elsbeth, a girl in her class. A lot of snow had fallen in Berlin that winter. It did not melt, so the street cleaners had swept it to the edge of the pavement, and there it had lain for weeks in sad, greying heaps. Now, in February, the snow had turned into slush and there were puddles everywhere. Anna and Elsbeth skipped over them in their lace-up boots.

They both wore thick coats and woollen caps which kept their ears warm, and Anna had a muffler as well. She was nine but small for her age and the ends of the muffler hung down almost to her knees. It also covered up her mouth and nose, so the only parts of her that showed were her green eyes and a tuft of dark hair. She had been hurrying because she wanted to buy some crayons at the paper shop and it was nearly time for lunch. But now she was so out of breath that she was glad when Elsbeth stopped to look at a large red poster.

"It's another picture of that man," said Elsbeth. "My little sister saw one yesterday and thought it was Charlie Chaplin."

# Observation in the Creation of the Children's Book Narrative

Experiences shape us; without them we would be empty shells. However, perhaps making a conscious decision about what to externalise is part of what determines writers and illustrators. There is also the question of the ability to remember and retrieve one's own experiences. It would seem that some of us have a natural predisposition to observation and laying down detailed memories while some people attach little value to this. As someone who remembers intricate details about their own childhood, it always surprises me when people say they have few early memories; we all experience but we don't all observe.

Many successful children's authors write stories based on their own experiences and perhaps these are the easiest to write. In order to empathise with a child it is important to think like one and there is no better way of transporting oneself into the mind of a child than the memory of childhood experience.

Judith Kerr's *'When Hitler Stole Pink Rabbit',*[16] is a good example of this translation of childhood feelings and emotion. Although this book was not published until Kerr was in her 40s, her narrative recreates the poignancy of her childhood experiences fleeing Berlin in the Second World War:

*'Elsbeth was getting annoyed. "Well then," she said "if you look the same as everyone else and you don't go to a special church, how do you know you are Jewish? How can you be sure?" There was a pause. "I suppose…….." said Anna, "I suppose it's because my mother and father are Jews, and I suppose their mothers and fathers were too. I never thought about it much until Papa started talking about it last week."'*[17]

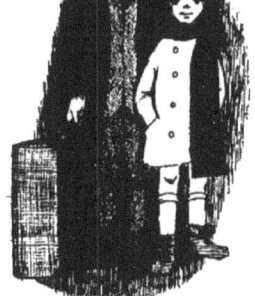

*Illustrated by the author*

It is not just the real life narrative that can be stimulated by observation. In his lecture at Anglia Ruskin University, Anthony Browne described the process of story making as '*Taking something which you have experienced and transforming it*'.[19] In his picture book '*Gorilla*', the main character Hannah is disappointed to receive a toy gorilla for Christmas.[20] But the toy changes into a real gorilla who takes her to exciting places while her father doesn't have time for her. In his interview for the Guardian, Browne says the idea grew from two separate experiences:

*'The first was a childhood birthday. I'd longed for a trumpet, a real one, but when I woke in the night and opened my present, I found this shiny plastic version. I remember the disappointment, vividly. And the second was a little boy in the village I used to live in. His parents had split up, and he was living with his mother. He could only have been about four, but he wandered the village, and practically every day he'd knock on my door, dressed in his Superman outfit. I think he saw me as a father figure, and it made me think about loneliness – the way Hannah looks for a father'*[21]

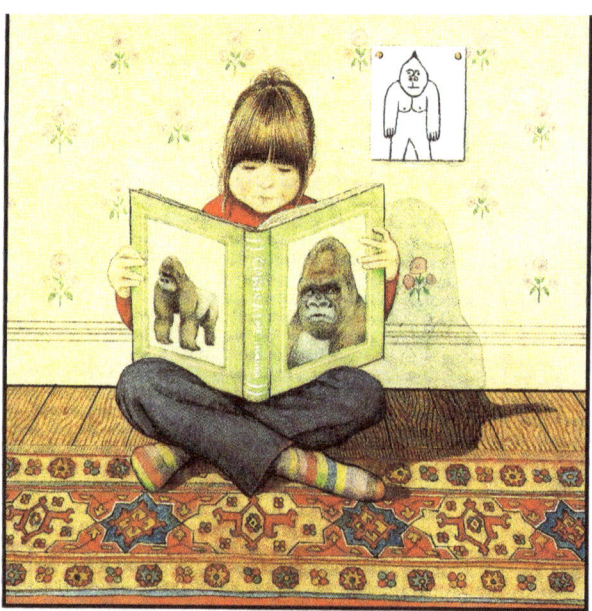

Hannah loved gorillas. She read books about gorillas, she watched gorillas on television, and she drew pictures of gorillas. But she had never seen a real gorilla.

Her father didn't have time to take her to see one at the zoo. He didn't have time for anything.

A good story idea is often based on the most simple observation, like the uncomplicated text of '*Lucy and Tom's Day*' by Shirley Hughes:

'*Once upon a time there were two little children called Lucy and Tom. This is a picture of them in the early morning. Lucy is big enough to get out of bed and put on her slippers and her red dressing-gown. Tom sleeps in a cot. He throws all his toys out, one by one-bump-onto the floor.*'[23]

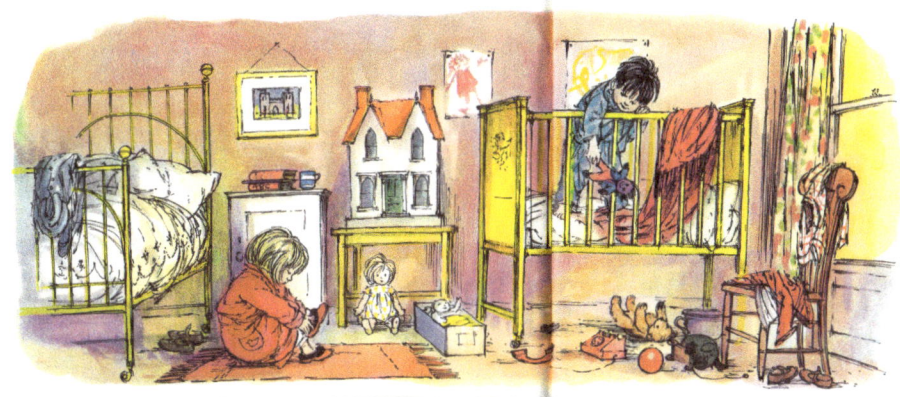

Once upon a time there were two little children called Lucy and Tom. This is a picture of them in the early morning. Lucy is big enough to get out of bed and put on her slippers and her red dressing-gown. Tom sleeps in a cot. He throws all his toys out, one by one —bump—on to the floor.

*LUCY AND TOM'S DAY by Shirley Hughes (Picture Puffins 1973)*
*Copyright © Shirley Hughes, 1960. With permission from Penguin Books Ltd.*[24]

Shirley Hughes comments on the creation of these simple narratives:

'*The people and places, though imaginary, needed to be contemporary and essentially recognisable. I wanted them to communicate a powerful sense of reality to the small child reader*'[25]

Sometimes a narrative that one believes to be imaginary will turn out to have an observational root, only becoming evident after its creation. Recently, chatting about a family boating holiday (when we found ourselves leaving a river and heading out to sea!) I realised where the idea for '*The Mouseboat*' had come from. When I spoke to the author illustrator Paula Metcalfe, she agreed:

'*A lot of my inspiration comes from real life. Things that I've seen/heard, things that have happened to me, emotions that I've experienced – all of these sneak into my narratives. But, they are normally mixed with a lot of imagination too. My first book 'Norma No Friends' was about a girl who was incredibly shy. For most of my teens and 20's I had a social phobia so the story was autobiographical in a way, although I didn't purposely set out to write about myself. It's often when I look back on a story that I notice it's about me or my friends/family.*'[26]

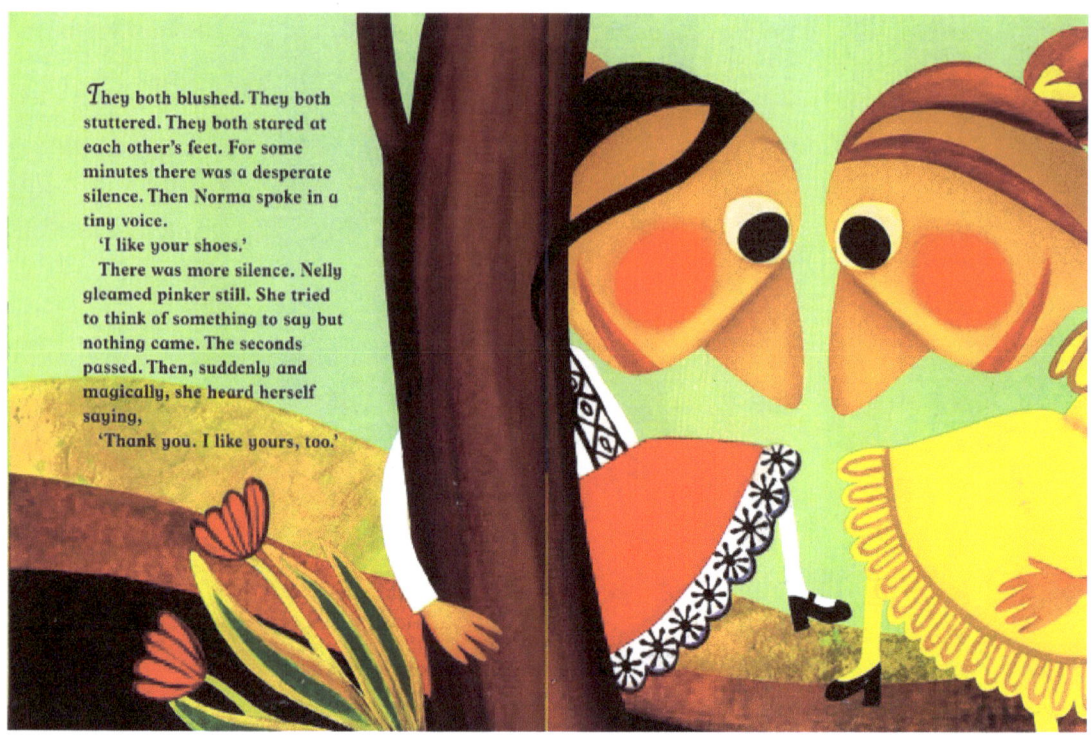

They both blushed. They both stuttered. They both stared at each other's feet. For some minutes there was a desperate silence. Then Norma spoke in a tiny voice.

'I like your shoes.'

There was more silence. Nelly gleamed pinker still. She tried to think of something to say but nothing came. The seconds passed. Then, suddenly and magically, she heard herself saying,

'Thank you. I like yours, too.'

*'Norma No Friends' by Paula Metcalfe, Barefoot Books Ltd 1999. Used with permission.* [27]

The simplest narrative is the wordless picture book where the pictures speak for themselves. The pictures may have to work harder, but hinge on the success of the narrative idea.

When Raymond Briggs created his wordless book *'The Snowman'* the simplicity of the story was key:

*'...so I dug this thing out of my files – it had been in there for about six years – this idea of a snowman coming to life: nice and simple, clean and silent.'* [28]

In his interview with Briggs, Benjamin Secher observes:

*'The simplicity of the story (a boy makes a snowman which comes to life and takes him on a magical flight through the night sky) only serves to heighten the tragedy of its ending: when the boy wakes up the morning after, the snowman has been reduced to a puddle.'* [29]

That such an iconic book can be borne of such a simple observation is testament to the importance of the observed in the creation of the narrative. The ability of the successful story maker to carefully observe and remember the detail of experience creates a mental sketchbook to be drawn upon whenever inspiration demands.

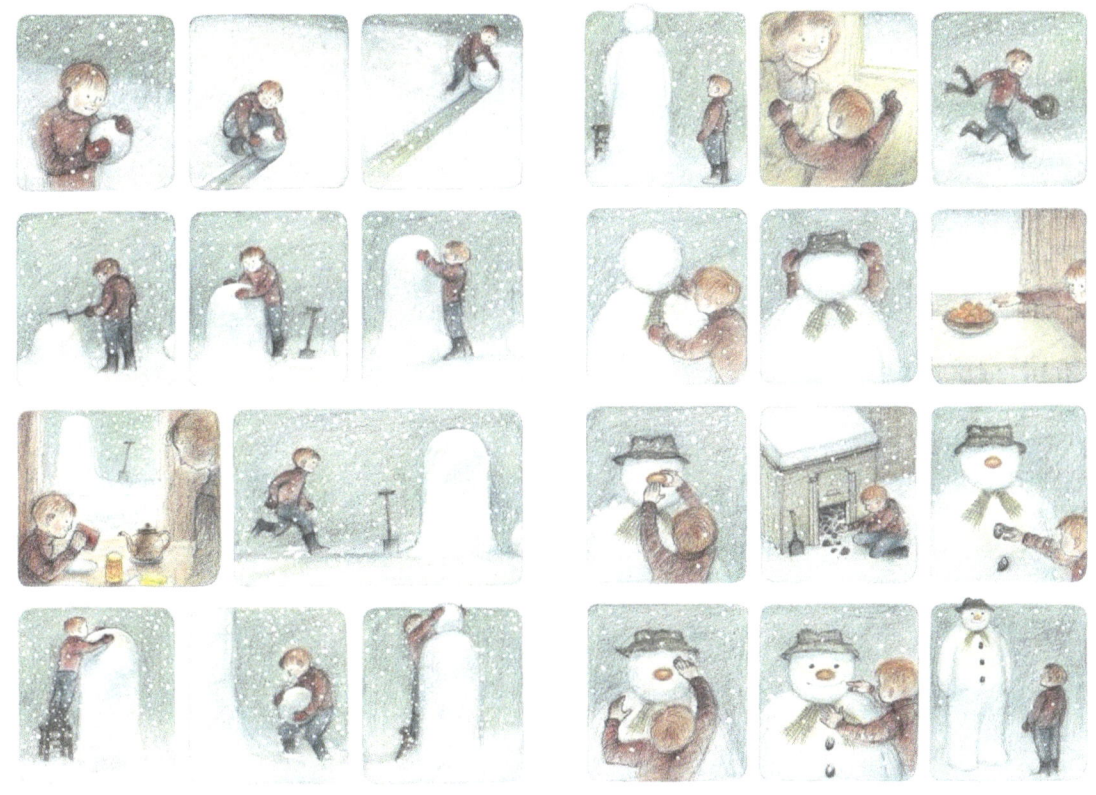

*THE SNOWMAN by Raymond Briggs (Puffins 1982)*
*Copyright © Raymond Briggs, 1982. With permission from Penguin Books Ltd.*

30

I like to create my own narratives, appreciating the freedom to be able to modify text as pictures evolve. But I have learned that the words don't always have to come first.

In a tutorial Pam Smy described the constraints of a rigid narrative *'like illustrating a greetings card'*; if the words come first, there will always be the temptation to render only what the words say. Creating a narrative after the images is more likely to allow the pictures to speak for themselves. The text becomes secondary, fulfilling a supporting role.

In the making of the narrative, this may give an author who is also an illustrator the edge. David Hughes comments: *'The act of drawing produces the idea'*

31

Drawing what is around you and making the narrative fit the pictures is a practice I have seen others achieve successfully. The advantage to this approach is that a sense of place is firmly established in the first instance leading to the creation of a convincing backdrop. One strong  example of this was created by Children's Book Illustration MA student Ashley Crowley in his picture book *'Baby Eats Book'*. During a concentrated and sustained period of observation of his own son Frankie, Crowley documented the life of a baby. Out of this grew a simple narrative successfully complementing rather than competing with the images. Crowley described the process which led to the emergence of the story:

*'Through drawing, I studied my child's movement and development in his first few months. Sketchbook after sketchbook I naturally began to see a sequence of images emerge which communicated his skills, behaviour and gestures in a visual narrative'*
[32]

This successful outcome reinforces the benefits to the illustrator of arriving at a narrative in this way, when one is already comfortable in the practice of observation.

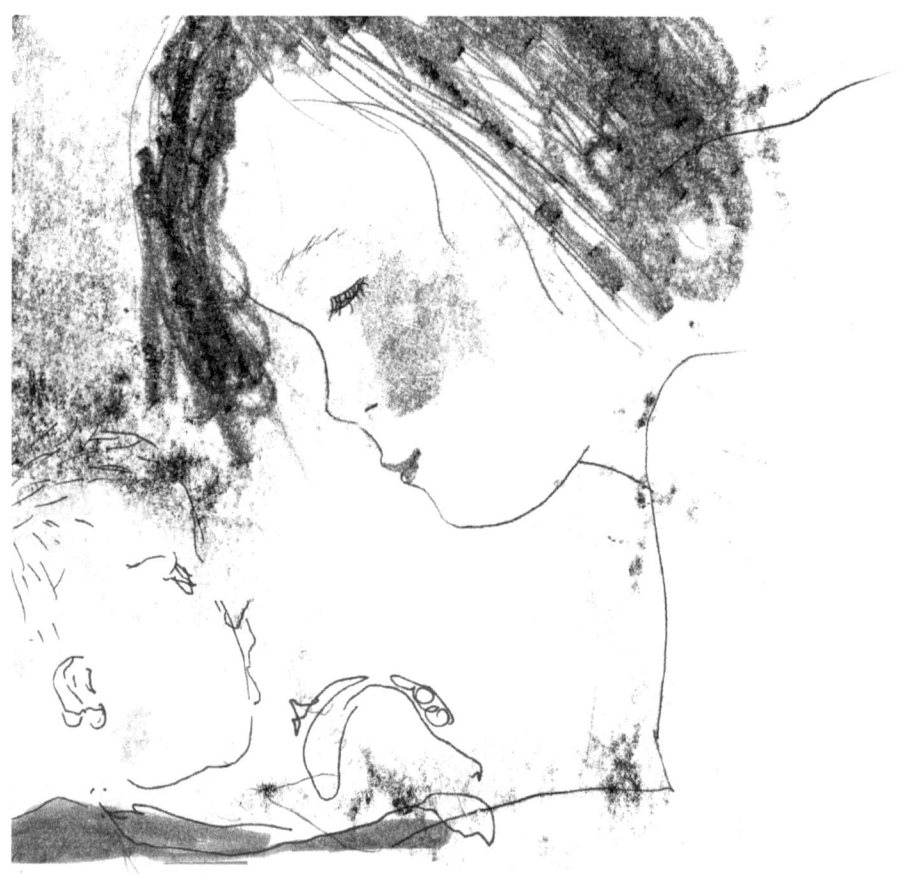

*'Baby Eats Book' by Ashley Crowley, 2010* [33]

Another important consideration when creating a narrative, is that of audience suitability. My picture book  *'Grandad'*[34] was based on my own childhood relationship and was written to help children deal with bereavement. The narrative was a very emotional journey for me. Friends who read it to their children also had an emotional response and it seemed to strike a chord with their own experiences. Although this book did prove a successful project, I did worry that the outcome may have represented a journey of self indulgence rather than something children would like to read. As a vehicle for adults to approach the subject of death it was not necessarily portrayed in a way that children or their parents would wish.

One parent told me *"My heart sinks every time she picks up that book because I know I will cry when I read it."*

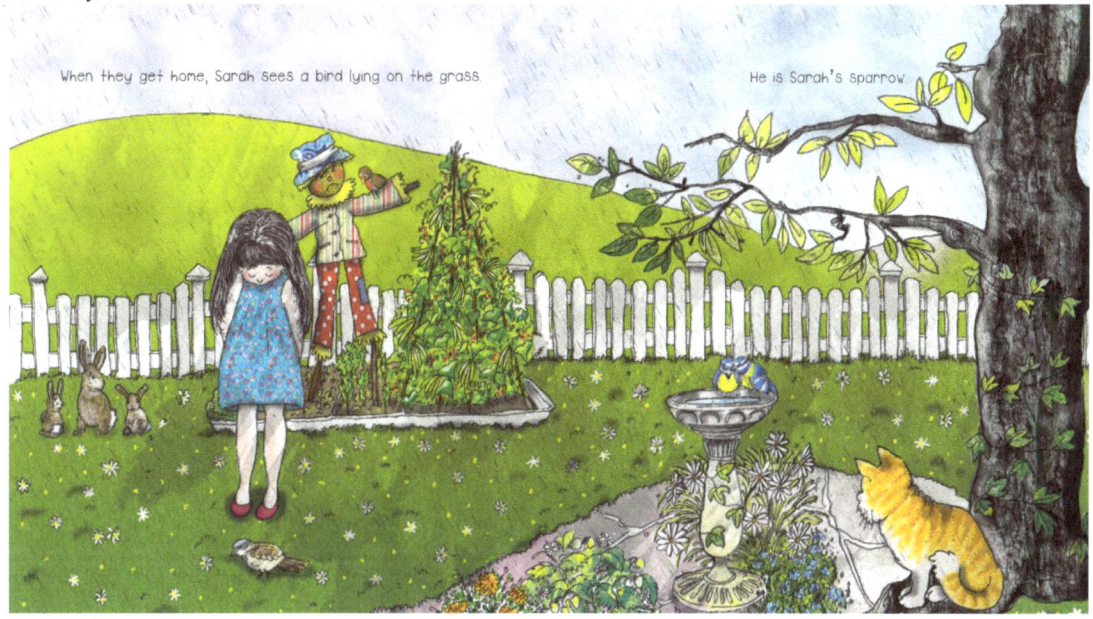

When they get home, Sarah sees a bird lying on the grass.

He is Sarah's sparrow.

*Grandad: A story to help children cope positively with bereavement,*
*Copyright © Sarah Hewitt, CreateSpace 2016* [35]

This humbling experience led me to wonder how I could become more in tune with the needs of my audience. In their article *'Wondering with Children: The Importance of Observation in Early Education'*, Foreman and Hall suggest five reasons to observe children:

*If I watch the children play, I can discover their interests.*
*By observing children, I can assess their developmental levels.*
*I look to see what strategies children use to attain their goals.*
*Observing children helps me know what skills the children need to practice.*
*When I observe children at play, I learn a lot about their personalities.* [36]

Whilst Foreman and Hall are referring to observation in the context of educational theory (as a vehicle for teachers to gather information about child behaviour), I believe these five points are also worthy of consideration by the story maker. Creating a narrative for children must surely begin with an observation of the child themselves. There is little merit in making a story which takes no account of what interests a child or is beyond their comprehension; one must try to understand their needs. A childhood book can make an impression that will last a lifetime so story makers have a huge duty of care. By observing children in this way, it is also possible to gain a deeper understanding about the essence of the child and not just the way they 'look'. If we have a deep understanding of children and their behaviour this must surely help with all aspects of creating books for children.

Through my research into the relationship between the creation of the narrative and the process at many levels, I spoke to writer and illustrator Alexis Deacon about his creative process and I feel his response encapsulates what observation offers in the story making process:

*'I think every story I have ever written has had some inspiration from the real world. It must have. But it is also possible to go 'fishing' for inspiration by putting yourself in front of things you know you respond to. I used to go to the zoo a lot to watch the different animals go about their business because I found that particularly good for making me think of stories. I'm sure it varies from person to person. If you keep your eyes and ears open a story can suggest itself at any time.'*[37]

*My son Christopher from a sketchbook*

# Observation and Narrative Non-fiction

The pedagogical concept that pictures can help to make learning fun is not new. Delivering facts to children in an exciting and attractive way can aid the learning process which can and should be a pleasure.

As children's illustrators we have the ability (and responsibility) to make learning pleasurable. In an article written for the Guardian, literacy expert Nicola Morgan describes the best young non-fiction as being defined by two things, usually together:

*'Illustration that grabs readers visually, and writing that hits the part of the brain where we respond deeply to language. This combination helps children learn to think, fostering a spirit of enquiry.*[38]

One of my earliest encounters with illustrated non-fiction was the Ladybird Book. These little books were full of realistic imagery, created in their familiar style. The pictures were very appealing to me and did help me to learn. They also led to a desire to draw things exactly as they are; something I am only just starting to shake off!

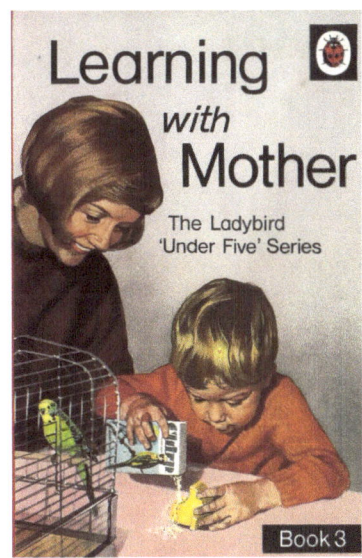
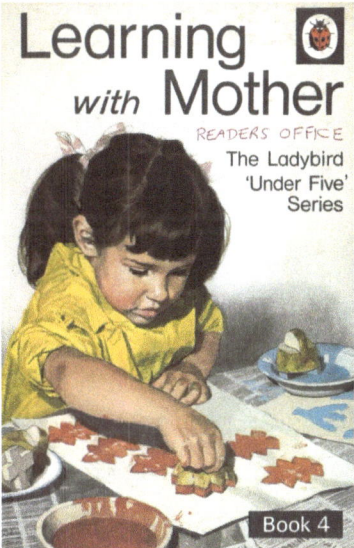
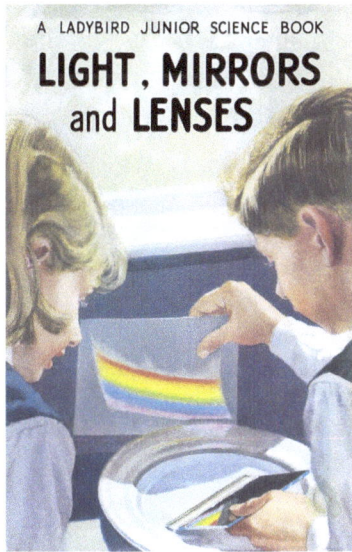

*Illustration from Learning With Mother: Book 3*
*© Ladybird Books Ltd., 1970*
39

*Illustration from Learning With Mother: Book 4*
*© Ladybird Books Ltd., 1971*
40

*Cover of Light, Mirror and Lenses*
*© Ladybird Books Ltd., 1962*
42

*Ladybird book covers (illustrations by Harry Wingfield)*

Looking critically at these books, the illustrations seem rigid and posed (probably as much to do with the era of their publication as the quality of the artwork).

Harry Wingfield illustrated many Ladybird titles including the *'Key Words Reading Scheme'* and *'Junior Science Series'* and his visual language is identifiable and consistent, being adopted as the house style for Ladybird. In his obituary, comment was made regarding the large collection of picture clippings he had amassed as a commercial artist prior to working for Ladybird. There was a suggestion that this was the reason for the photographic quality of his images.

The use of photographs as a tool for observation is a contentious one; most would agree that there is no substitute for drawing from life. Joining the MA course, many of us admitted to drawing from photographs but following the observational module, we can now see why this may not be ideal. Observation from life is about the whole picture. One cannot get a feel for the life and vibrancy of a subject from a flat image, nor the very personal experience of seeing something for oneself. Intricacies such as texture, colour, scale and character can all be distorted by a camera. If the photograph has been taken by someone else, one's own observation may be further inhibited by the creative interpretation of another.

Often when illustrating for a non-fiction title however, drawing from life is not always possible and photographs are an invaluable source for accurate reference. Whether this can be classified as observation is questionable, but if an illustrator is in the habit of observational drawing, the use of photographs to inform is a useful tool. Taking one's own photographs to supplement observation may be useful. If one has learnt to draw through observation, then a photograph will inform without the need to meticulously copy.

Author illustrator Marta Altés told me:

*'I don't usually draw from photographs, but sometimes I've had to. When you have a project due 'yesterday', photographs are good. I remember when I had to illustrate an article that talked about the different benches of Barcelona and I was living in the UK, photos were the only solution.'*[42]

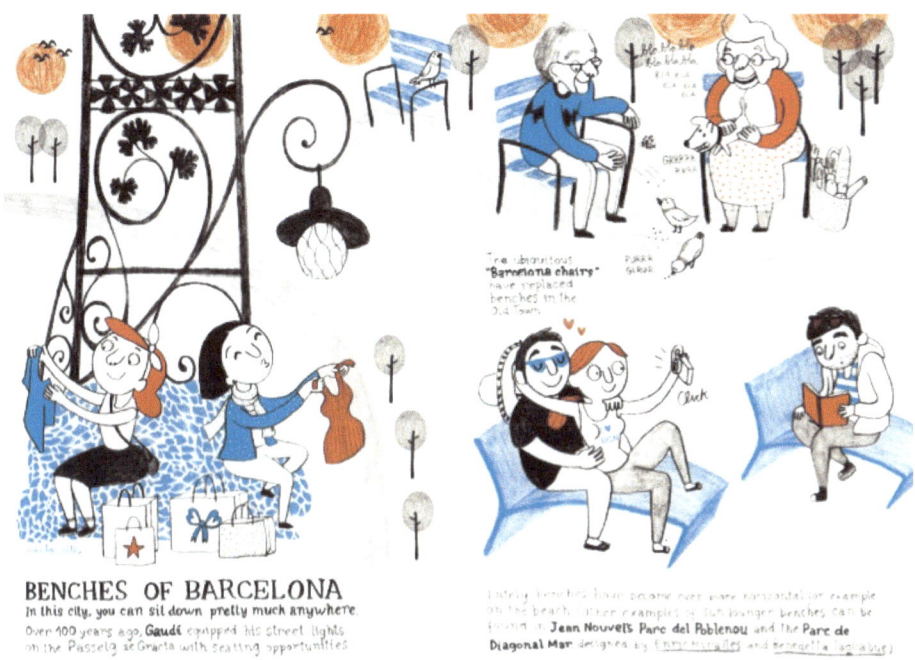

*'Benches of Barcelona' by Marta Altés used with permission* [43]

Somehow, the idea of illustrating non-fiction never seems to feel as exciting as the fictional narrative and fellow students on the MA course don't often choose a non-fiction subject for their projects. I spoke to them about why they thought this might be. Elena Arevalo commented:

*'It is an area which has not had much of an outing in our course, but this perhaps is because we are being encouraged to be authors of our own books and in the vast majority of our projects we have gone for the most imaginative and personal quests.'*

Daisy Hirst summed this up:

*'If it is non-fiction you don't get to decide that an elephant fell out of the sky'.*

It is important at this point to draw a distinction between non-fiction books where function is primarily to educate and present facts, and what may be described as 'narrative' or 'literary non-fiction'. In an article entitled *'What is literary non-fiction?'* The School of Journalism and communication describes the genre:

*'Writers commonly use the techniques of fiction, including creation of a narrative arc, character development, scene-setting, action sequences, dialogue and interior monologue. The true stories they write using these techniques have the drama of fiction and force of fact. Literary non-fiction takes shape in many forms, from reportage to memoir, from personal essay to biography. Nature writing, travel writing and science writing all have their literary practitioners.'* [44]

Martin Salisbury argues that *'the best non-fiction illustration can be both informative and visually stimulating'*, defining and being aware of narrative non-fiction may open up more opportunities for creativity, character development and drama.[45]

A good example of narrative non-fiction is the picture book *'Anne Frank'* written by Josephine Poole and based on Anne Frank's diary. Illustrated by Angela Barrett, this book would surely disprove any assertion that non-fiction is the poor relation of fictional texts. The beautiful and evocative illustrations bring the tragic true story to life.

I spoke to Angela Barrett about the creation of the illustrations and asked her how observation had played a part; everything seemed so well observed, with a strong sense of place and time. I had assumed she had made much observational drawing in preparation.

Her first reaction was to question what observation was in this context; she felt that the process would be better defined as *'research'*. Barrett explained that she rarely goes out and draws, and at art school never ventured into the life room. When she came to start work on *'Anne Frank'* she didn't visit the house where the events took place, nor did she do much in the way of preparatory drawings, referring only to photographs for context. She said she was wary of visiting the house in case she then was unable to create her own vision of it in her illustrations:

*'There is a danger with drawing from observation that the results will be too fresh and obsessive, that one loses all sense of freedom and expression and inhibits imagination and the ability to express emotions.'*[46]

Barratt told me that the only observational drawing she made for the book was for the illustration of a cloakroom where she hung up her own coat to see how the folds fell. On studying the finished image, one realises that there are errors in perspective and proportion. For example, the ceiling appears far too low and the figures are short and distorted. While this may have been avoided with greater use of observational drawing, it is these 'errors' which bring focus, drama and character to the illustration. The low ceiling renders the space the children occupy close and oppressive, while the distorted features of the children's faces emphasise the intensity of the scene.

Barrett said that she has always used memory drawings. This enforces the idea explored in the previous chapter suggesting some people are more predisposed to the retention of detailed memory and experience. It would seem that Barrett is able to translate her memories into successful visual imagery, observing in detail almost subliminally and creating a memory bank of material for future use in her illustrations, dispensing with the need to physically draw from observation.

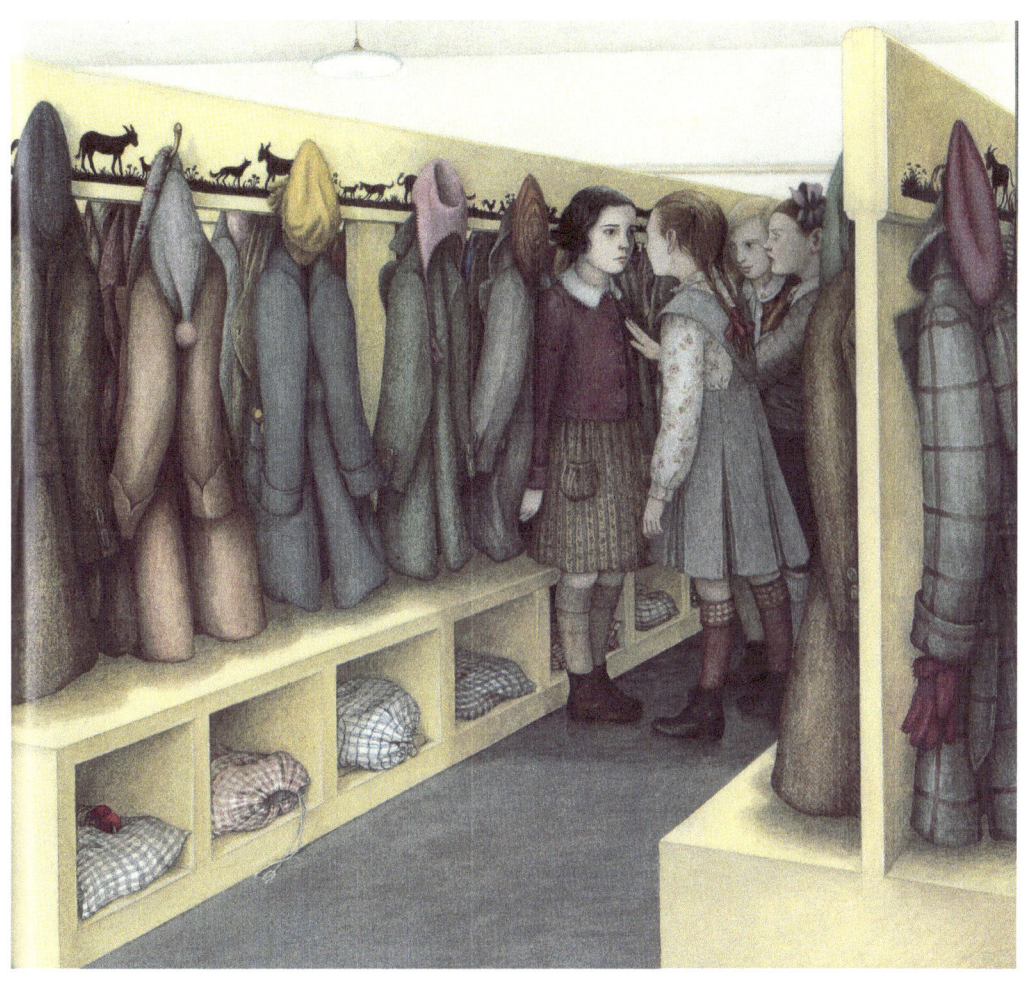

*From Anne Frank by Josephine Poole  published by Hutchinson 2005.*
*Illustration © Angela Barrett, 2005.* [47]
*Reproduced by permission of The Random House Group Ltd.*

Her ability to create the evocative and atmospheric illustrations in all of her work also stems from a memory. When she was a child she had a treasured book of Russian fairy tales with dark and atmospheric backgrounds. Following a traumatic house fire, the book survived, but then was given away by her mother. The disturbing event and the fact that the book was lost, honed her memories of the illustrations and left Barrett *'drawn to gloomy atmospheres'*

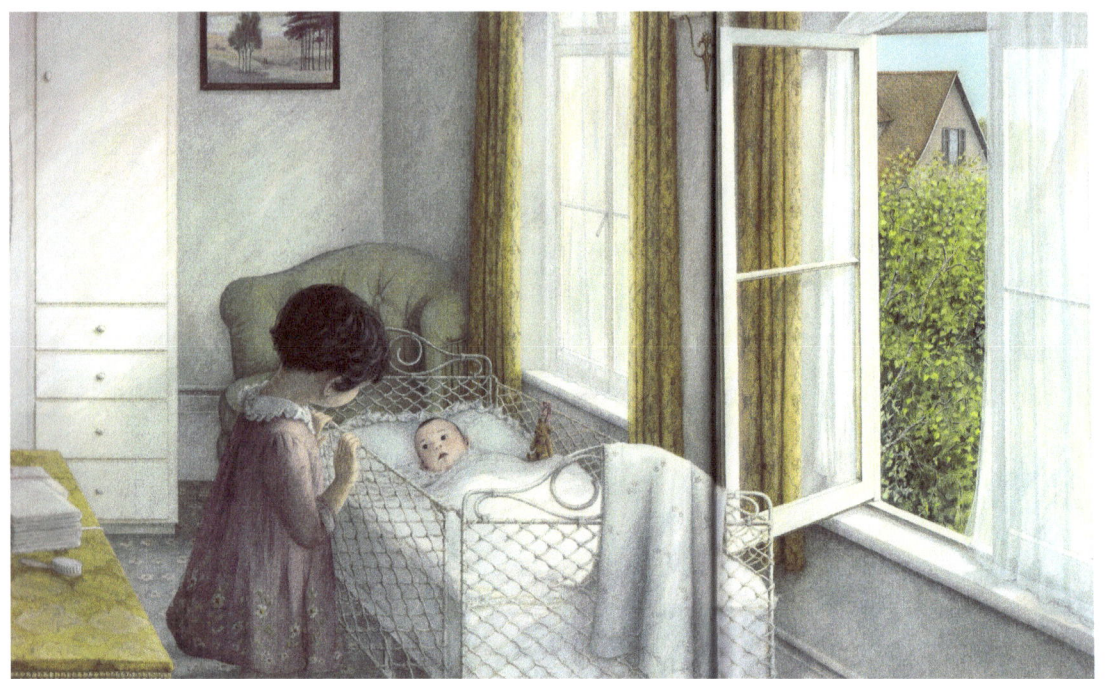

The second project on the MA course was called the '*Sequential Image*'. I decided to work on a narrative non-fiction subject. '*Clara*' [49] is the story of an 18th century Asian rhino who was taken by her owner on a tour of Europe.

I chose to create a wordless picture book and so the story needed to be easily understood just by looking at the pictures. It was a huge task, and apart from the idea of using the genre of Rajput painting as an inspiration (a genre contemporary to Clara's story), I wasn't sure where to begin.

I discovered that there were some baby Asian rhinos at Whipsnade, so one bright, Autumn day I went and sat overlooking their enclosure sketching.

Drawing and observing the rhinos gave me a unique insight into their character;  how they move, their gesture, their playfulness, their intelligence and other subtleties such as how the colour and texture of their skin appears to alter with changes in light. Sketching them over and over that day and observing whilst not necessarily drawing, informed much more than my resourced photographic references.

*i. Rajput painting, also known as Rajasthani Painting, is a style of Indian painting, evolved and flourished during the 18th century in the royal courts of Rajputana, India.*

*From my sketchbook, Nepalese baby rhino, Whipsnade*

I was able to start drawing immediately with reference to my observational sketchbook research and more crucially from my own memory. These memory drawings allowed me to be free from the constraints of copying an already posed image and allowed Clara to do whatever my imagination willed her to. The study of Rajput painting and other Indian art, observed but not copied, also led to the creation of a visual language which worked well with the subject matter.

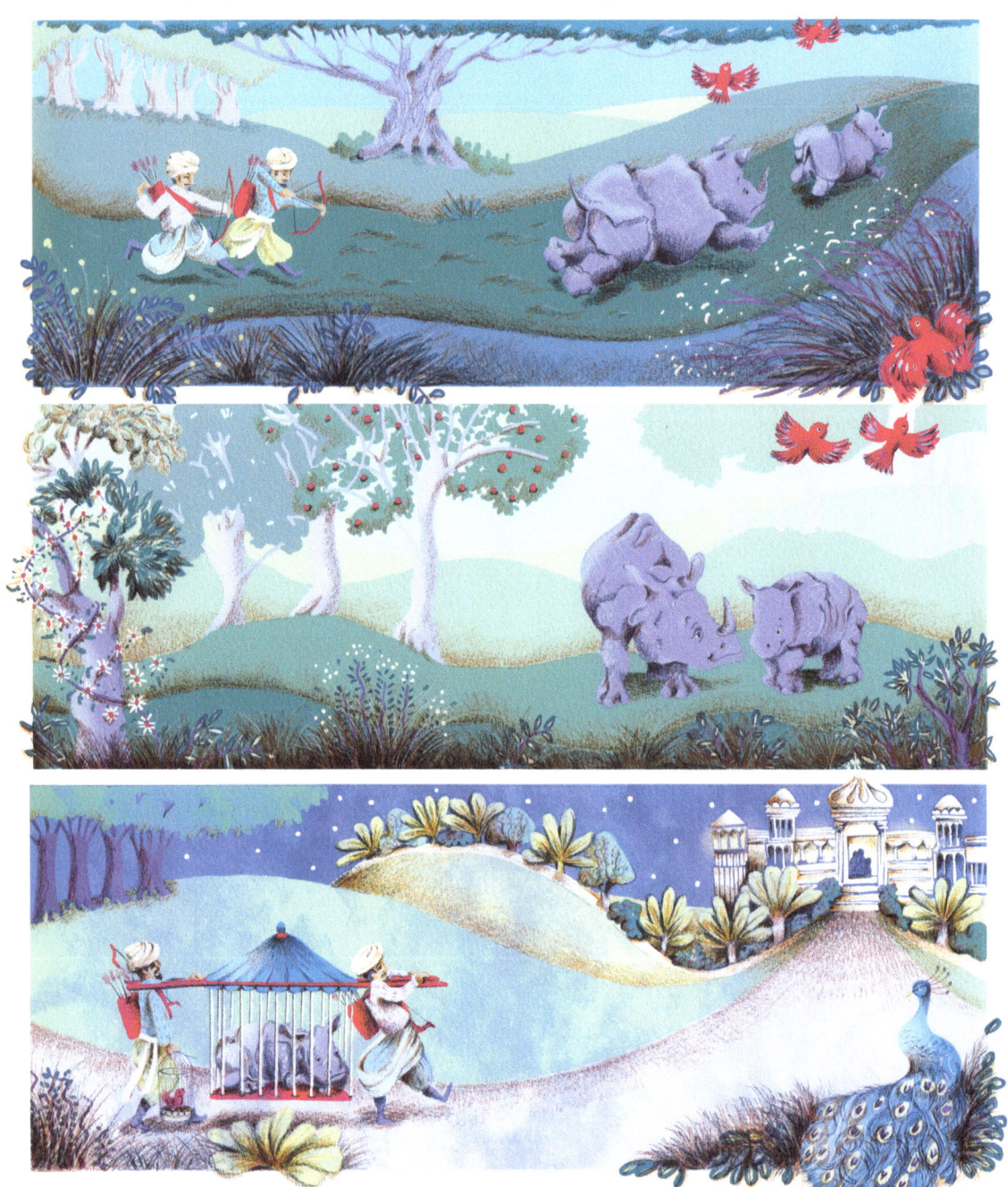

*Clara: The True Story of Clara the Rhino,*
*Copyright © Sarah Hewitt, CreateSpace 2016*

Knowing that I was illustrating a true story did create additional considerations leading to the requirement for research into objects, people, places and events but I tried to ensure this was used only as reference material rather than copied and placed awkwardly within a composition.

Working on *'Clara'* was my first experience with the creation of a stylised image and the finished outcomes were detailed and complex. However, narrative non-fiction doesn't have to be a complex production; it can work with even the most simple stylised imagery. For the younger child it may be argued that this simple approach is particularly suited as it focuses the reader's attention where complex pictures may create distractions. The author-illustrator Geoff Waring illustrates with flat, stylised imagery which *'keeps my pictures bold and simple – almost like having scissors and coloured paper to make a collage'.*[51]

Waring's use of flat shapes and colours reminds me of why, arriving on the MA course, we felt observational drawing was not terribly important to us. One might assume that these images were created with little or no reference to life, but in his biography for his publisher Walker Books, Waring says:

*'As an illustrator, I have always illustrated ideas, and have hundreds of sketchbooks to prove it. My first books are based on my own cat, Oskar, who I missed when we went to live in Sydney for two years, so I created him as a cartoon.'*[52]

It is not clear whether the ideas in his sketchbooks were drawn directly from life or from memory, but they were certainly derived from Waring's own experience. As well as memories of his pet, things learned in childhood pursuits of bird watching and *'messing about in ponds'* are also present in his subject matter and text.

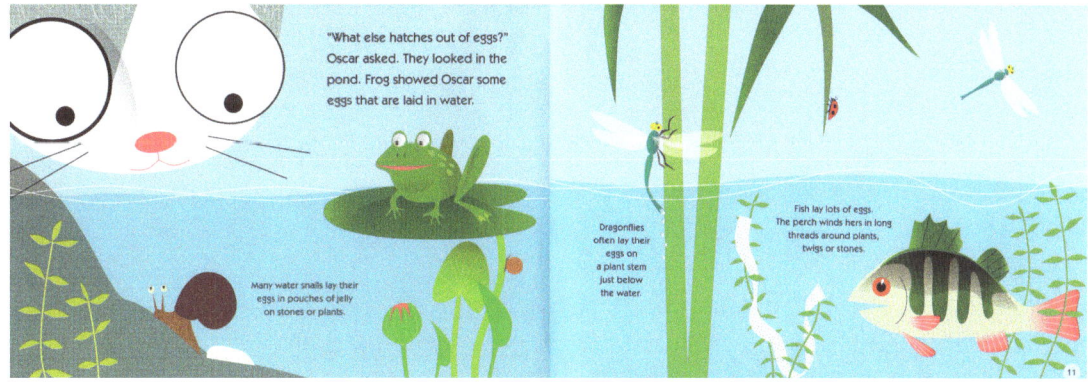

This practice of observation leading to informed imagination is something which I am only just beginning to comprehend. In my next chapter I will explore this process further.

Working on education publications in the role of illustrator or art editor (where illustrations are often prescribed and contrived to fulfil the text), had given me a very blinkered opinion about the opportunities non-fiction could offer the illustrator. However, what I have discovered through working on *'Clara'* and through my research, is that there is nothing boring about illustrating non-fiction.

If I had decided to present *'Clara'* as a simple factual account, I would not have had the opportunity to create the character that Clara became. Within the wordless narrative I was able to create an imaginary world based on the facts of real events and places which allowed the story to be brought to life creatively. For someone like me who struggles with the imaginary, the true story gave me a starting point on which to build. Observational drawing, research and the exploration of different factual events led me to the creation of my own narrative, characters and imagery, set apart from the actual events that occurred. The observation of fact in the context of narrative non-fiction can open up exciting possibilities:

*'Whatever you call it, it is a form of storytelling as old as the telling of stories. The genre recognises both the inherent power of the real and the deep resonance of the literary.'*[54]

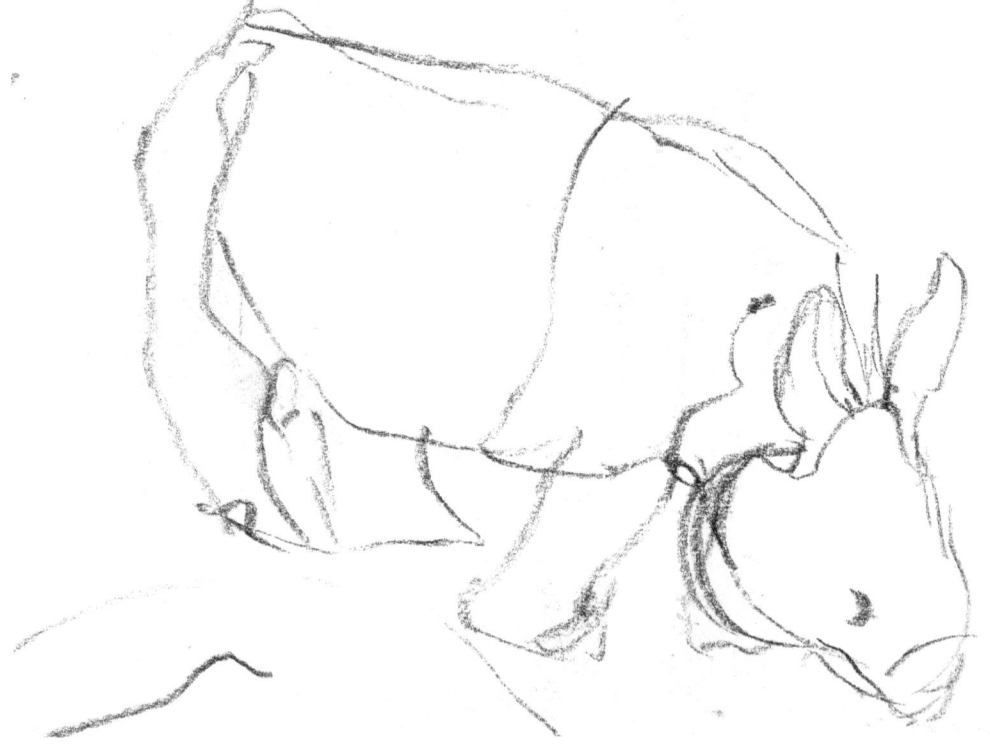

# Observation Leading to Informed Imagination

One of the most difficult processes for me as I learn how to create illustrations for children, is transforming what I see in to imaginary. However, I am finding that when I stimulate this creative process by drawing from reality, sometimes good ideas will follow. When I was looking for an imaginative cover illustration for *'Clara'*, the idea evolved directly from a sketch of a rhino I had made from life at Whipsnade. An adult rhino stood, completely filling a doorway, the rectangle of the door framing the animal and emphasising its scale:

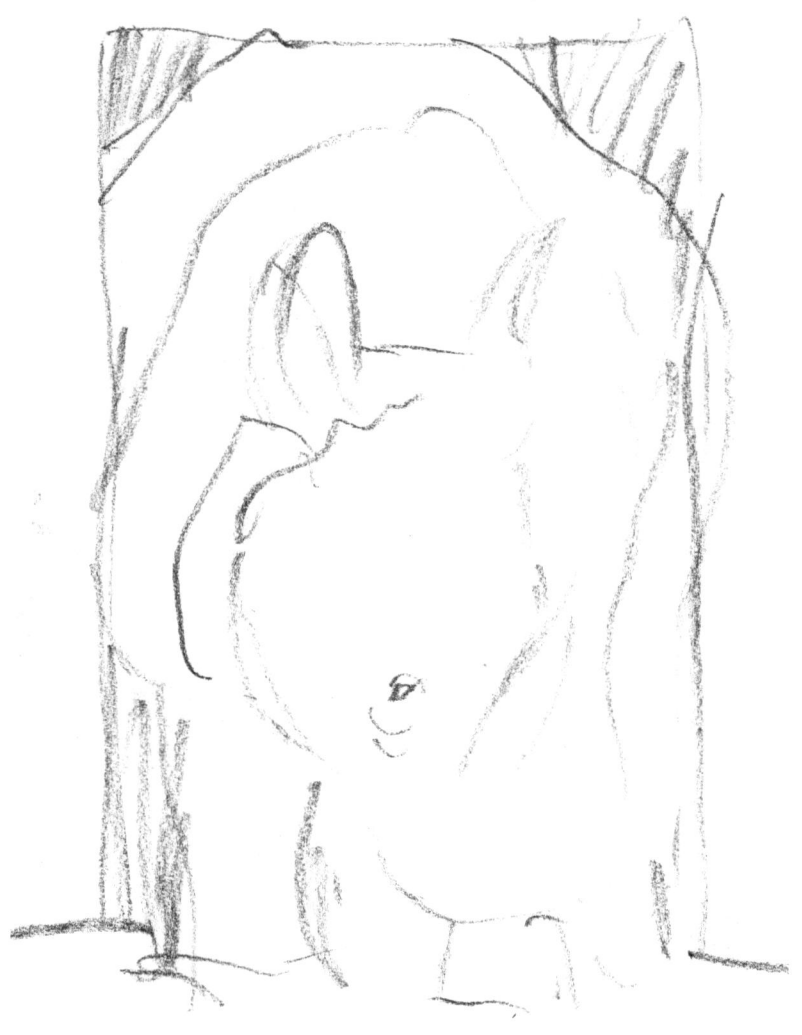

*Sketch of adult Nepalese rhino, Whipsnade*

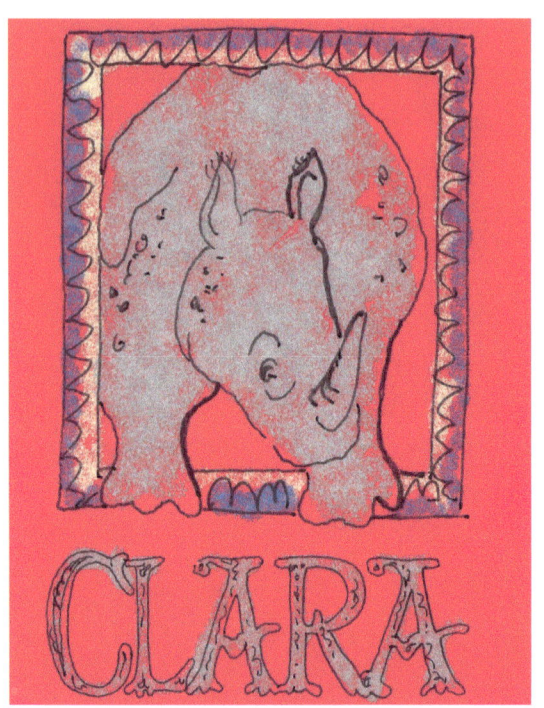
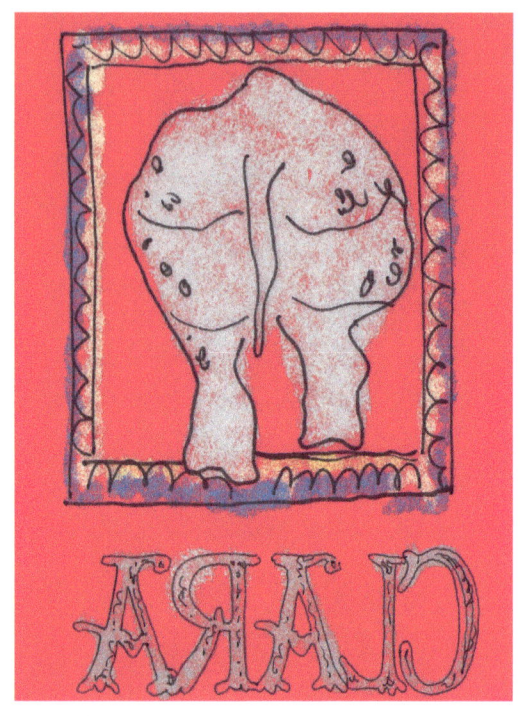

*Developmnent for cover design*

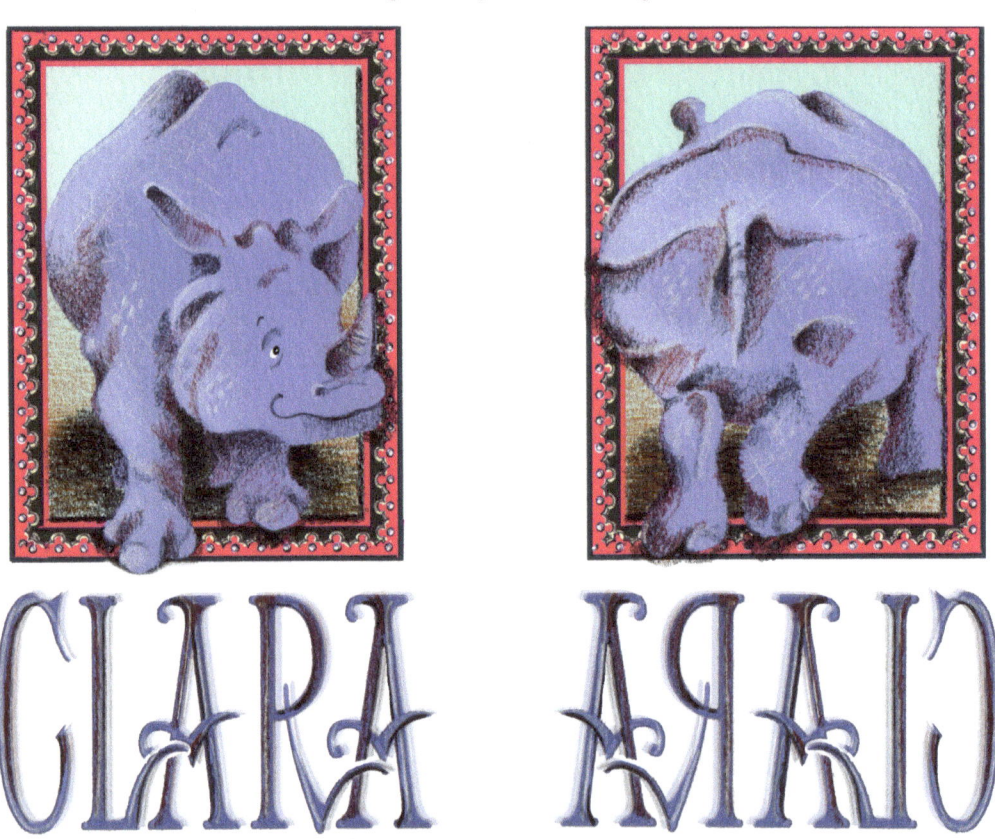

*Finished cover design*

34

The reflection of Alexis Deacon on his experiences drawing in the Galapagos Islands describes this process of observation leading to informed imagination:

*'The power that drawing has to give solid form to the imagination has been a source of endless fascination to me. Gradually, I have come to understand how inseparable that world is from the 'real' world that surrounds and feeds it. For this reason (and a few others!) the trip to Galápagos was a fantastic chance ... I was as interested in what I would later forget or distort as what I could remember. In one way or another Galápagos has informed everything that I have done since.'*[55]

Deacon's work is always underpinned by meticulous observational study. His sketchbooks offer an insight into the way that the observed can transform into the imaginary; classically influenced life studies leading to characterisation, gesture and inflection, carefully observed. He explained to me the reason for his honed and practiced observational drawing:

*'When I was a teenager I believed that observational drawing and drawing from imagination were two entirely different things.That being so, I decided that I was definitely someone who drew from imagination and sort of gave up on observational drawing on principle. Later on I began to realise that observation was very far from being the opposite of imagination. There were certain things that I wanted to be able to draw, figures and faces mainly at that time, that I began to understand I would never be able to render convincingly without looking at them and trying to discover how they worked. That process gave me a new passion for observation because the transformation in what I was able to draw after I had undertaken it was so marked (unsurprisingly)'*[56]

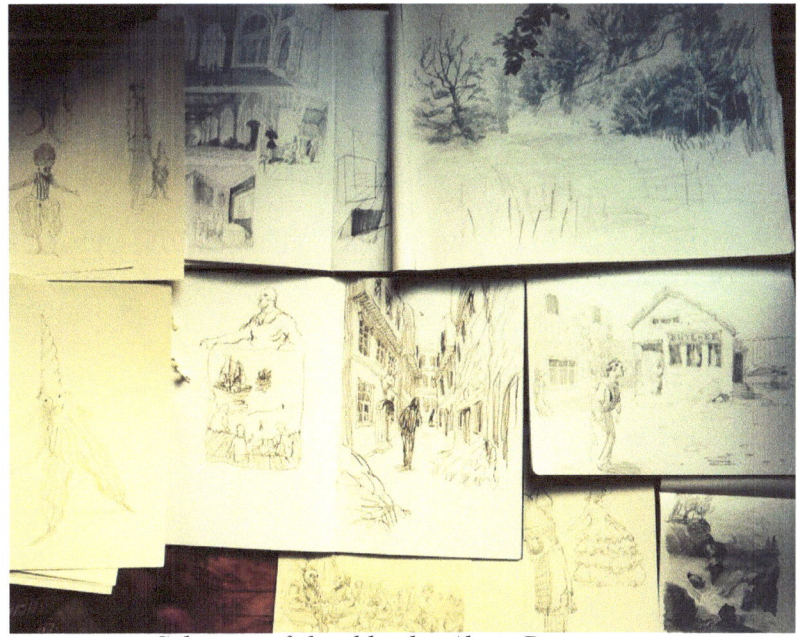

*Selection of sketchbooks, Alexis Deacon*

Following his time drawing in the Galápagos, Deacon produced the picture book *'Croc and Bird'*. The imaginary world the creatures inhabit was inspired by his journey. The sense of place and the vibrancy of colour and light create life, movement and atmosphere, all informed by his experience, lending an imaginary place a credible reality.

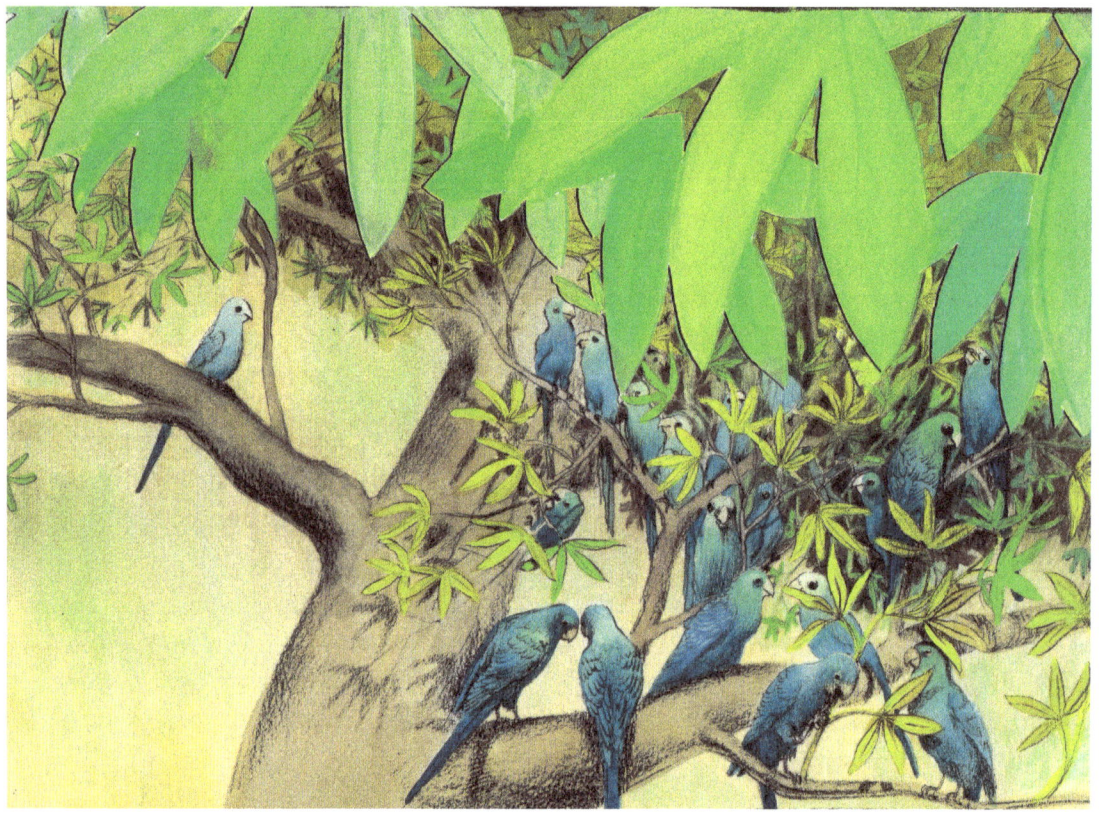

*From Croc and Bird by Alexis Deacon  published by Hutchinson 2012.*[57]
*Copyright © Alexis Deacon, 2012. Reproduced by permission of The Random House Group*

Exploring the relationship between observation and informed imagination led me to question whether it can extend to design and composition. In *'Graphic Design School Principles'* David Dabner describes the benefits of observational drawing to the designer:

*'Sketching and drawing engage you in a constant process of looking and aid in understanding the world around you. Observational drawing, or drawing used to document, makes you see the subject as a shape or shapes and colour as tones; it teaches you to understand and manipulate perspective, to understand how an object exists in space, and to create the illusion of space and depth of field.'*[58]

It is very easy to forget the importance of design when creating an illustration; sometimes I find it is just one thing too much to think about when there are so many other considerations, even though I have ten years experience as a graphic designer.

In his book *'Illustrating Children's Picture Books'* Martin Salisbury confirms that this is an area which is often overlooked by students. He emphasises the important role good composition can play[59]

*'The arrangement of shapes across a double page spread plays a key role in the way we read a pictorial sequence, both in terms of directing the eye and aesthetic balance.'*

On our MA course we learned that a good layout can do much to help with finished outcomes and should be fundamental at the planning stage. Composition, layout and perspective can influence mood pace, atmosphere and help to direct the attention of the audience; sometimes it is not so much about the space your illustration inhabits but the white space it does not.

I find that my design experience means that there is often a subliminal attention to composition, but I still work to hone a more conscious awareness. Where observation has influenced design it has been productive. Informing the colour palette for *'The Mouseboat'* and the cover design for *'Clara'* were two occasions where observation led directly to a finished graphic decision.

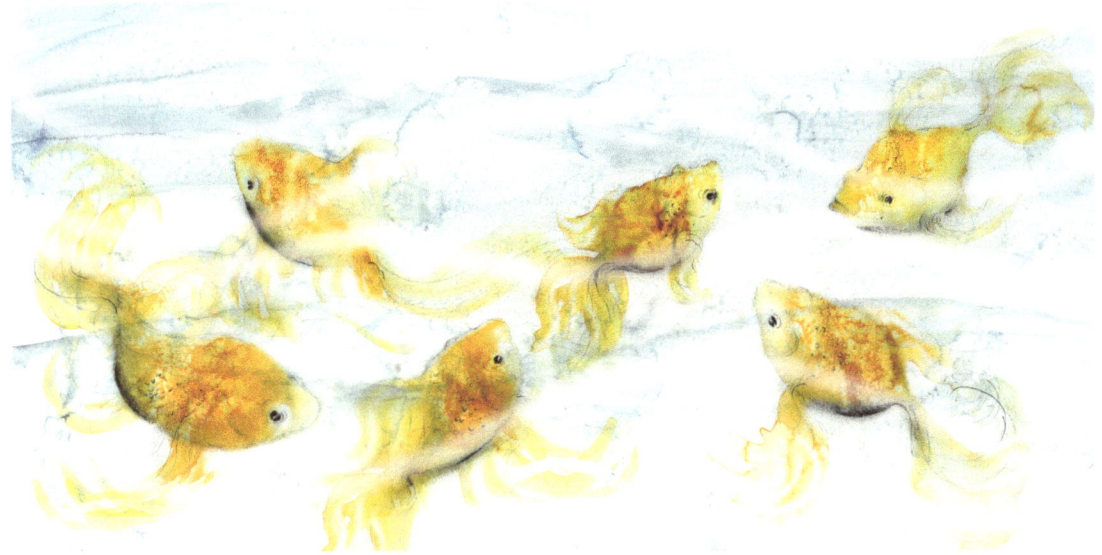

*'The Mouseboat': observation informing design and colour palette*[60]

The illustrator Helen Ward plans the design of her pages carefully and combines powerful graphic layouts with carefully observed illustrations. One can see how the observation of colours in nature has led to the creation of palettes such as the rich vibrant tones in her illustrations for *'The Cockerel and the Fox'* and the more subtle colours employed in *'The Hare and the Tortoise'*.

The natural forms of the animals create graphic shapes designed to fulfil functions such as leading the eye through the illustration, emphasis and pace. Like Angela Barrett, Ward's illustrations are a result of informed imagination:

*'I do draw from life sometimes, but sheep, for example, always end up on the other side of the field – I suppose they see me as a predator. So I simply observe and remember.'*[61]

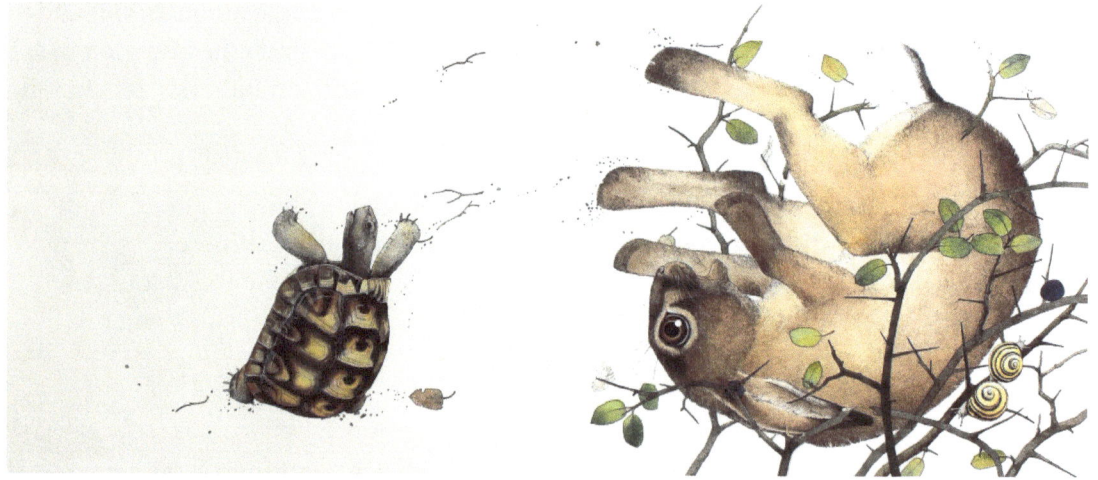

*From the Hare and the Tortoise by Helen Ward, Published by Templar Publishing*[62]

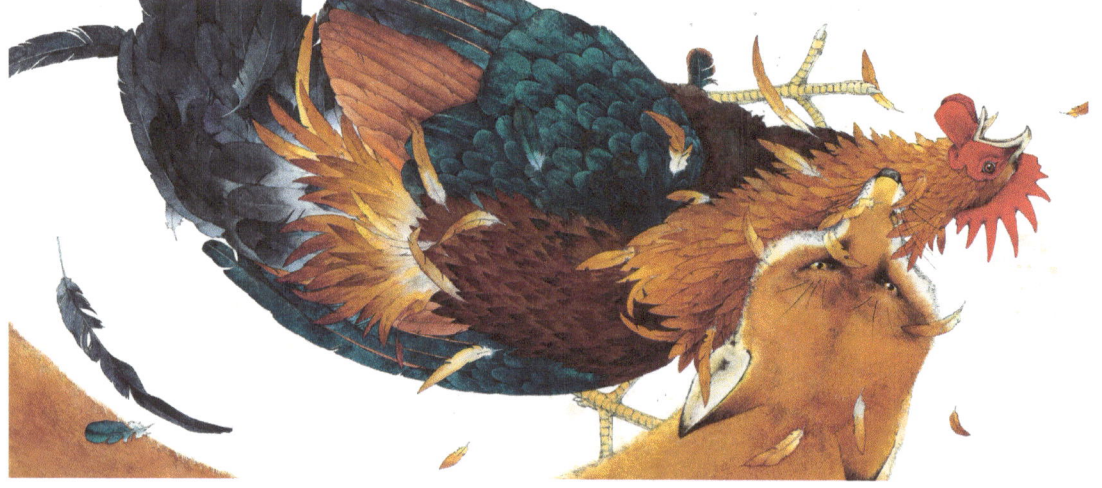

*From The Cockeral and the Fox by Helen Ward, Published by Templar Publishing*[63]

Children's illustrators often develop an imaginative and stylised visual language; their characters and the world they inhabit may look nothing like reality but what they represent still needs to be identifiable. Marta Altés whose illustrations are simple and stylised, told me about the development of her character for the children's book *'No'*. The character is not realistic or 'life like', but gesture, movement and basic characteristics define and identify it as a dog. [64]

*'I didn't have my dog with me when I drew it, but I did have him for 2 years, so I drew from my memory. And even though the drawings are not perfect, I think they catch the essence of the movement of a dog.'*

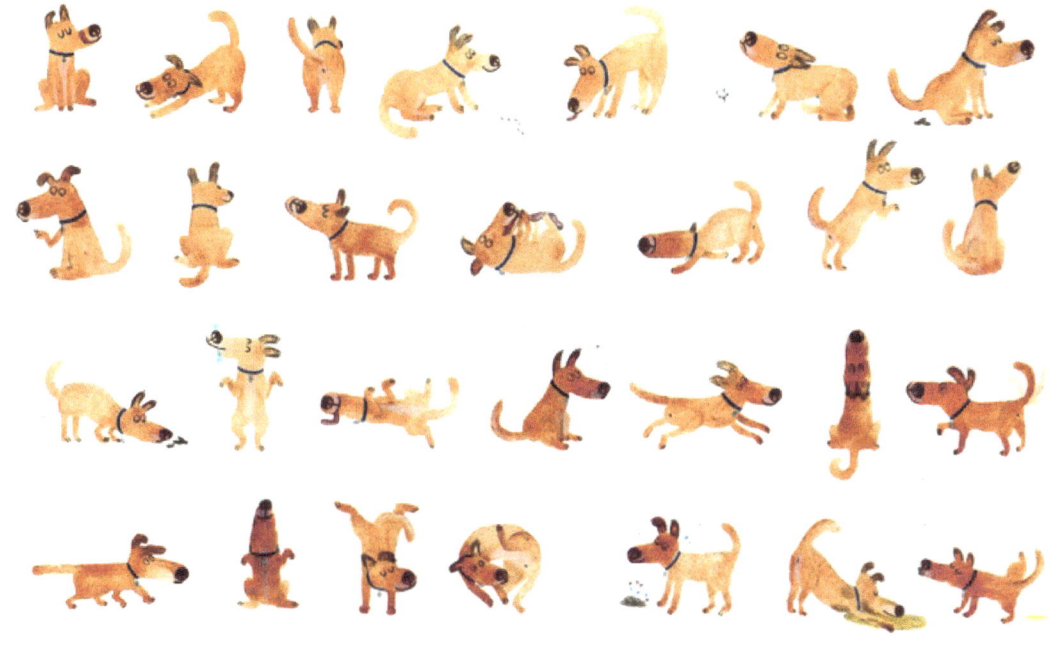

*Character Studies for 'No' by Marta Altés. Used with permission* [65]

Memory drawing, also mentioned by Angela Barrett, Alexis Deacon and Helen Ward, seems to set the illustrator free to be more imaginative enabling drawing with the benefit of remembered observation. Altés adds:

*I think I use observation for the character development unconsciously .... I just draw from memory, but if I need to use observation, I do it. I think it does help me. For example ....I was useless at drawing cats ... but unconsciously, now that I'm living in a house with a cat, suddenly I think my cats are getting better!'*

Author illustrator Paula Metcalf who, like Altés illustrates with a stylised visual language, told me:

*'I don't often use observation drawing when I work – practically everything comes from my imagination. But I am sure that a lifetime of being fascinated by people, animals, faces, emotions, relationships, colours and countryside has stocked my imagination with material, so what I do is a kind of observation drawing.'*

[66]

Metcalf told me that she immerses herself in the imaginary by putting herself in the position of the character, empathising with them and imagining their facial expression by wearing it on her own face:

*This is never conscious, but sometimes after a particularly challenging drawing my face aches, and I realise it's because I have been making the expression that I need my character to wear!'*[67]

I have often done this myself and it usually happens when one forgets the physical process of drawing: those perfect moments when it becomes the action of the subconscious mind. The instance of becoming the character allows an empathy at a level beyond that of the outsider looking in. Perhaps this is observation taken to its deepest level and imagination is the formulated observation of one's own thoughts.

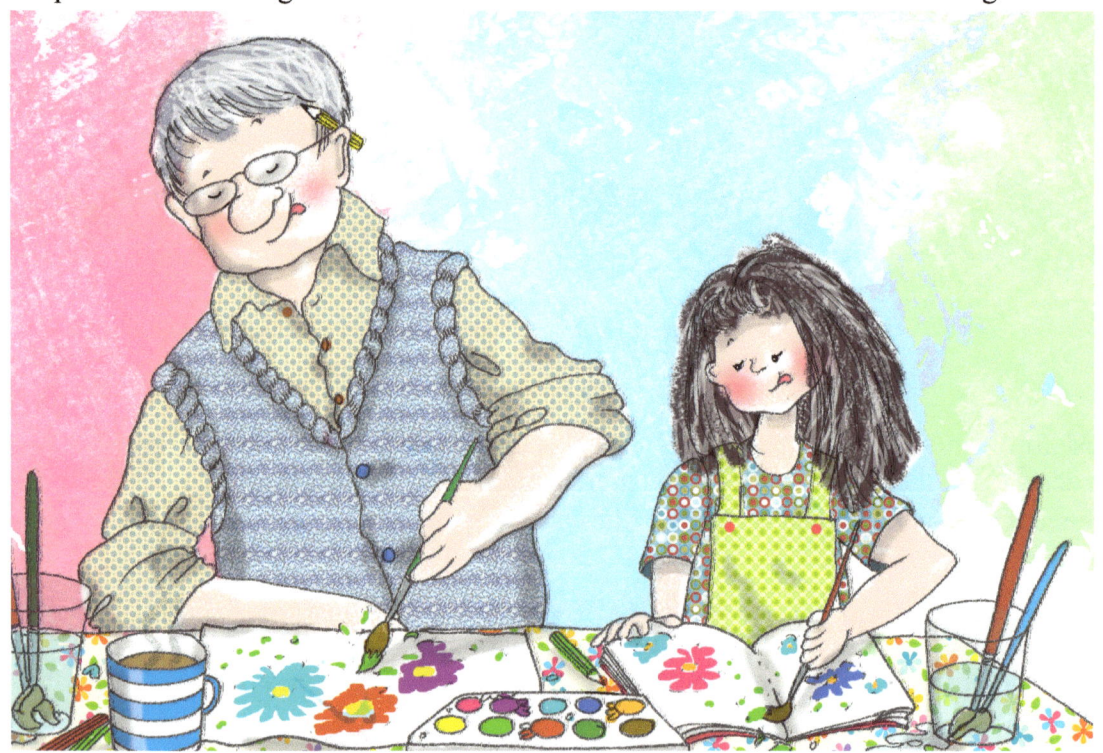

*Grandad: A story to help children cope positively with bereavement, Copyright © Sarah Hewitt, CreateSpace 2016*[68]

# Conclusion

Through the generosity of my tutors and chosen illustrators, who have all been willing to share their experiences, opinions and insights with me, I have explored a variety of working practices in the context of the role that observation plays in the creation of books for children. It has also been an opportunity to reflect and discuss my own development as an illustrator and in a broader sense, how I have seen, see and will see the world.

By examining my own practice I have learned that observation is a vehicle for unlocking imagination and an essential starting point. Observation can be instrumental in the creation of the first idea, the development of the narrative, composition, colour, design and many other areas yet to discover.

These conclusions are as much about developments in my own practice as about the title of the study, realising that observation has already filtered into my work even when I have not made a conscious decision to include it.

It is clear that how we remember and observe defines us as creative people and perhaps more precisely as children's story makers. Observing the world through the eyes of a child is something that people who write and illustrate for children often have an innate predisposition to do. That is not to say that children are an unsophisticated audience; we know that they are capable of interpreting images at a level way beyond their reading age. As a volunteer helper at my own children's primary schools, I often observed young children confidently making sense of complex pictures. Knowing this reinforces the idea that as writers and illustrators, a pedagogical approach to the observation of children may inform us about what they respond to and their sophisticated demands as our audience.

While Edward Ardizzone claimed to reject the process of observation, affirming that illustrators were stimulated by text and imagination, his regular practice of drawing from life, surely filtered into the marks he made as an illustrator. Informing his practice with reference to other artists and illustrators, where techniques and effects mastered were observed and transfused into his work, uniquely rendered but still informed by his observations. This is something that illustrators often do subliminally because we are interested in how others make their pictures. The observation and discussion of the work and working practice of fellow students on the Children's Book Illustration MA along with visiting published illustrators, has had a huge influence on the development of my own illustration techniques, ideas and practice.

Angela Barrett was keen to point out that her observations may be better described as references. But the way she studies the world and remembers what she sees may nevertheless be defined as a form of observation. When Paula Metcalfe wears the expressions of her characters on her own face, imagining as she draws, she is bringing the imaginary into the physical form and placing her imagined observations onto paper for her audience. However abstract the outcome, observation can inform even in at a most basic level, with considerations such as light, colour and design.

We are all shaped by our experiences of the world, our observations about relationships, what we see, what we feel, and what it is to be human. By transporting ourselves into imaginary situations we can use our informed imagination to create believable scenarios and images; we can learn how to fool our audience convincingly. Understanding the role of observation means we can manipulate what we observe to suit our needs and as a tool to further our own practice.

I have learned that children's story makers personalise the tool of observation. For Angela Barrett, equipped with an innate ability to look and record, the step of drawing from life is bypassed completely, while Alexis Deacon feels observational drawing is essential in order to be equipped to adequately express his imagination.

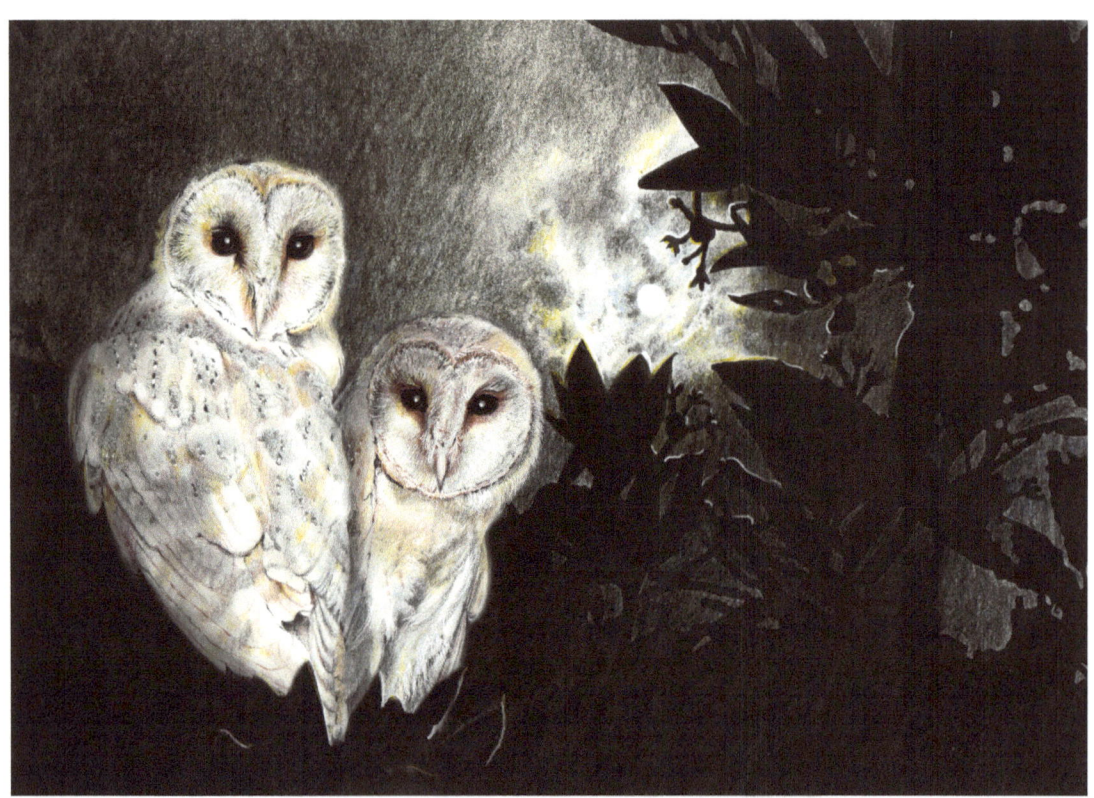

*From my book 'The Sleeping Garden'*[69]

Whether we start with observational drawing and let it lead us to the narrative, or observe a seed stored deep within our minds as Raymond Briggs did when he created the *'The Snowman'*, it is observation that leads us to understand and empathise. Once we are comfortable with what we know and understand, our confidence to transcend reality will lead us deeper into the imaginary. When I decided to explore observation in children's book creation, I already suspected that the role it had to play was extensive. However, discovering the sheer scale of infiltration into the creative process has made me question the direction of my work and empowered me to strive for greater goals.

I have discovered that the role observation plays is a supportive one, underpinning, informing and leading to all creative decisions. Learning about the way the illustrator can utilise and exploit observation as a tool has raised my aspirations for creation, while reassuring me that the practice of observation can stimulate and support my future practice and lead to solutions in all areas of the creative process.

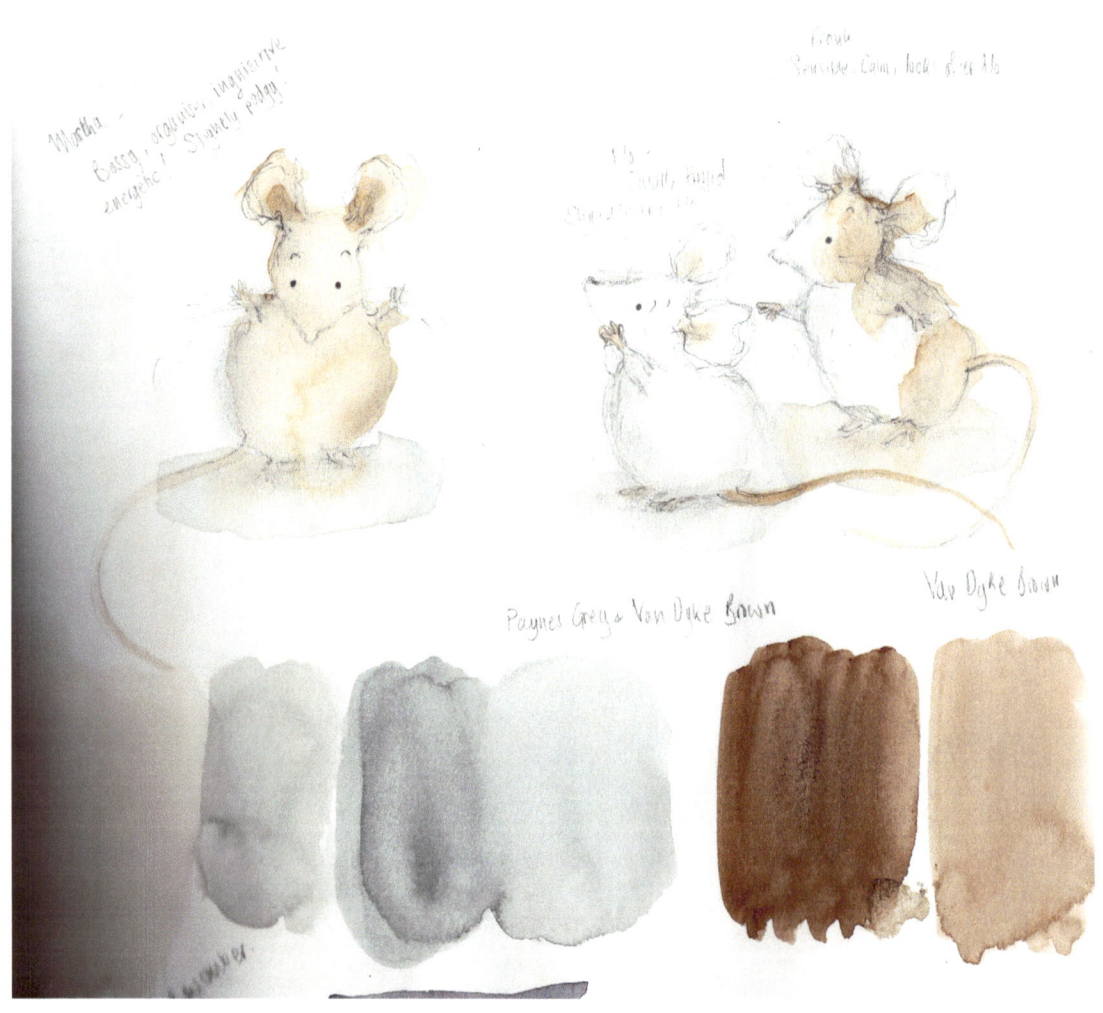

*From my sketchbook 'The Mouseboat'*

# References

1. Lovoos, M., Drawing : A Search for Form  p.57 Reinhold Publishing Corporation 1965

2. Hughes, S., A Life Drawing p.207 The Bodley Head London 2002

3. Dorne, A., Famous Artists Magazine Winter Famous Artists Schools, Inc 1963

4. Ardizzone, E., Diary of a War Artist The Bodley Head 1974

5,6,7. Ardizzone, E., The Born Illustrator  http://www.edwardizzone.org.uk/motif accessed 1st March 2012

8. Hewitt, S., The Mouseboat

9. Potter, B., The Tale of Two Bad Mice Frederick Warne & Co 1904

10. Hewitt, S., The Mouseboat

12. Hughes, S., Letter to Sarah Hewitt 3rd March 2012

13. Hughes, D., Email discussion with Sarah Hewitt February 16th 2012

13. Smy, P., Pam Smy Illustrator http://pamsmy.blogspot.co.uk

14. Hughes, S., A Life Drawing pp. 184,185 The Bodley Head London 2002

15. Coates-Smith,W.,Salisbury,M., Line No2 Children's Books p32 APU Cambridge 2001

16. Kerr. J., When Hitler Stole Pink Rabbit Harper Collins Children's Books; July 2008

17. Kerr. J., When Hitler Stole Pink Rabbit pp.6,7 Harper Collins Children's Books; July 2008

18. Kerr. J., When Hitler Stole Pink Rabbit p.5 Harper Collins Children's Books;  July 2008

19. Browne, A., Lecture at Cambridge School of Art, Anglia Ruskin University 2010

20. Browne, A., Gorilla London:Walker Books 2002

21. Crown, S., A life in books: Anthony Browne interview for The Guardian Saturday 4th July 2009

22. Browne, A., Gorilla London:Walker Books 2002

23,24. Hughes, S., Lucy and Tom's Day Penguin Books Ltd 1973

25. Hughes, S., A Life Drawing p.169 The Bodley Head London 2002

26. Metcalfe, P., Email discussion with Sarah Hewitt  February 16th 2012

27. Metcalfe, P., Norma No Friends Barefoot Books 1999

28,29.Secher, B., Raymond Briggs: I don't believe in happy endings The Telegraph 24th December 2007

30.Briggs, R., The Snowman Puffin;1982

31.Hughes, D., Studio presentation at Cambridge School of Art, Anglia Ruskin University February 2012

32,33. Crowley, A., Email discussion with Sarah Hewitt  5th April 2012

34,35. Hewitt, S., Grandad: A story to help children cope positively with bereavement Copyright © Sarah Hewitt, CreateSpace 2016

36. Forman, G., Hall, E., Wondering with Children: The Importance of Observation in Early Education Early Childhood Research and Practice http://ecrp.uiuc.edu/v7n2/forman.html http://ecrp.uiuc.edu/v7n2forman.html accessed 25th March 2012

37. Deacon, A., Email discussion with Sarah Hewitt March 22nd 2012

38.Morgan, N., Spirit of inquiry The Guardian Saturday 8th November 2003

39. Wingfield, H., Wingfield, E., Learning with Mother Book 3: The Ladybird Under Five Series Ladybird Books 1970

40. Wingfield, H., Wingfield, E., Leaning with Mother Book 4: The Ladybird Under Five Series Ladybird Books 1971

41. Newing, FE, Bowood, R., (authors) Wingfield, H., (illustrator)
LIGHT, MIRRORS AND LENSES (Series 621: A Ladybird Junior Science Book)
Ladybird Books. 1962

42,43. Altés, M., Completed questionnaire and supplied images dated April 9th 2012

44. University of Oregon School of Journalism and Communication, What is Literary NonFiction? http://Inf.uoregon.edu/whatis accessed 25th March 2012

45. Salisbury, M., Illustrating Children's Books p108 A&C Black Publishers 2004

46. Barrett, A., telephone interview with Sarah Hewitt April 2012

47,48. Poole, J., illustrated by Barrett, A., Anne Frank  A Hutchinson 2005

49,50. Hewitt, S., Clara: The True Story of Clara the Rhino, Copyright © Sarah Hewitt, CreateSpace 2016

51,52. Waring, G., Walker Books author biography http://www.walker.co.uk/contributors/Geoff-Waring-2736.aspx accessed 5th April 5th April 2012

53. Waring, G., Oscar and the Frog Walker Books 2007

54. University of Oregon School of Journalismn and Communication., What is Literary Non-fiction? http:/Inf.uoregon.edu/whatis accessed 25th March 2012

55. Galápagos Conservation Trust 2011., Alexis Deacon http://www.artistsvisitgalapagos.com/artist/alexis_deacon

56. Deacon, A., Email discussion with Sarah Hewitt March 22nd 2012

57. Deacon, A., Croc and Bird Hutchinson 2012

58. Dabner, D., Graphic Design School Principles p18 Wiley; 3 edition 2004

59. Salisbury, M., Illustrating Children's Books p120 A&C Black Publishers 2004

60. Hewitt, S., The Mouseboat

61. Carey, J., Animal Magic: Helen Ward interview for The Guardian Saturday 29th March 2008

62. Ward, H., Ward, P.E., The Hare and the Tortoise Millbrook Press 1999

63. Ward, H., The Cockerel and the Fox Templar Publishing; New edition 2004

64. Altés, M., Completed questionnaire dated April 9th 2012

65,66.Metcalf, P., Email discussion with Sarah Hewitt  February 16th 2012

68. Hewitt, S., Grandad: A story to help children cope positively with bereavement Copyright © Sarah Hewitt, CreateSpace 2016

69. Hewitt, S., The Sleeping Garden.

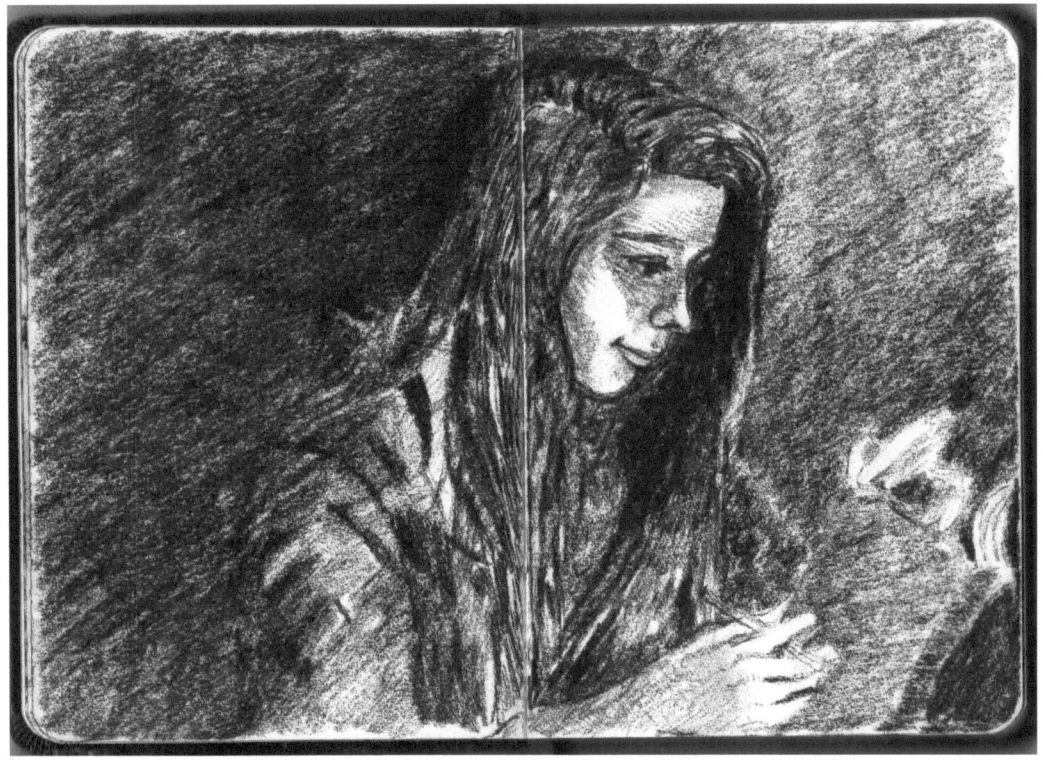

*From my sketchbook 'Observation and Experiment'*

# Bibliography

Altés, M.,Completed questionnaire and supplied images dated April 9th 2012

Ardizzone, E., Diary of a War Artist' © by Edward Ardizzone, Bodley Head 1974

Ardizzone, E., The Born Illustrator  http://www.edwardardizzone.org.uk/motif accessed lst March 2012

Barrett, A., telephone interview with Sarah Hewitt April 2012

Brigham Young University., Literary Worlds: Illumination of the Mind accessed 25th March 2012

Briggs, R., The Snowman Puffin; 1982

Browne, A., Gorilla London:Walker Books 1983

Browne, A., Lecture at Cambridge School of Art, Anglia Ruskin University 2010

Carey, J., Animal Magic: Helen Ward interview for The Guardian Saturday 29th March 2008

Coates-Smith, W., Salisbury, M., Line No1 Reportage APOU Cambridge 2001

Coates-Smith, W., Salisbury, M., Line No2 Children's Books APU Cambridge 2001

Crowley, A., Email discussion with Sarah Hewitt April 5th 2012

Crown, S., A life in books: Anthony Browne interview for The Guardian Saturday 4th July 2009

Dabner, D., Graphic Design School Principles Wiley; 3 edition 2004

Deacon, A., Email discussion with Sarah Hewitt March 22nd 2012

Deacon, A., Croc and Bird Hutchinson 2012

Dorne, A., Famous Artists Magazine Winter Famous Artists Schools, Inc 1963

Forman, G., Hall, E., Wondering with Children: The Importance of Observation in Early Education Early Childhood Research and Practice http:// ecrp.uiuc.edu/v7n2/forman.html" http://ecrp.uiuc.edu/v7n2/forman.html accessed 25th March 2012

Galapagos Conservation Trust 2011., Alexis Deacon http/www.artistsvisitgalapagos.com/artist/alexis _deacon accessed 5th April 2012

Hewitt, S., Clara: The True Story of Clara the Rhino, Copyright © Sarah Hewitt, CreateSpace 2016

Hewitt, S., Grandad: A story to help children cope positively with bereavement, Copyright © Sarah Hewitt, CreateSpace 2016

Hewitt, S.,, The Mouseboat 2012

Hughes, D., Email discussion with Sarah Hewitt February 16th 2012

Hughes, D., Studio presentation at Cambridge School of Art, Anglia Ruskin University February 2012

Hughes, S., A Life Drawing p.207 The Bodley Head London 2002

Hughes, S., Letter to Sarah Hewitt 3rd March 2012

Hughes, S., Lucy and Tom's Day Penguin Books Ltd 1973

Kerr, J., When Hitler stole Pink Rabbit Harper Collins Children's Books; New edition (July 2008)

Lovoos, M., Drawing: A Search for Form Reinhold Publishing Corporation 1965

Metcalfe, P., Email discussion with Sarah Hewitt February 16th 2012

Metcalfe, P., Norma No Friends Barefoot Books 1999

Morgan, N., Spirit of inquiry The Guardian Saturday 8th November 2003

Newing, FE, Bowood, R., (authors) Wingfield, H., (illustrator) LIGHT, MIRRORS ANDLENSES (Series 621 : A Ladybird Junior Science Book) Ladybird Books 1962

Poole, J., illustrated by Barrett, A., Anne Frank  A Hutchinson 2005

Potter, B., The Tale of Two Bad Mice Frederick Warne & Co 1904

Salisbury, M., Styles, M., Children's Picturebooks A&C Laurence King Publishing 2012

Salisbury, M., Illustrating Children's Books A&C Black Publishers 2004

Secher, B., Raymond Briggs: I don't believe in happy endings The Telegraph 24th March 2007

Smy, P., Pam Smy Illustrator http://pamsmy.blogspot.co.uk accessed 25th March 2012

University of Oregon School of Journalism and Communication., What is Literary Nonfiction? http://Inf.uoregon.edu/whatis accessed 25th March 2012

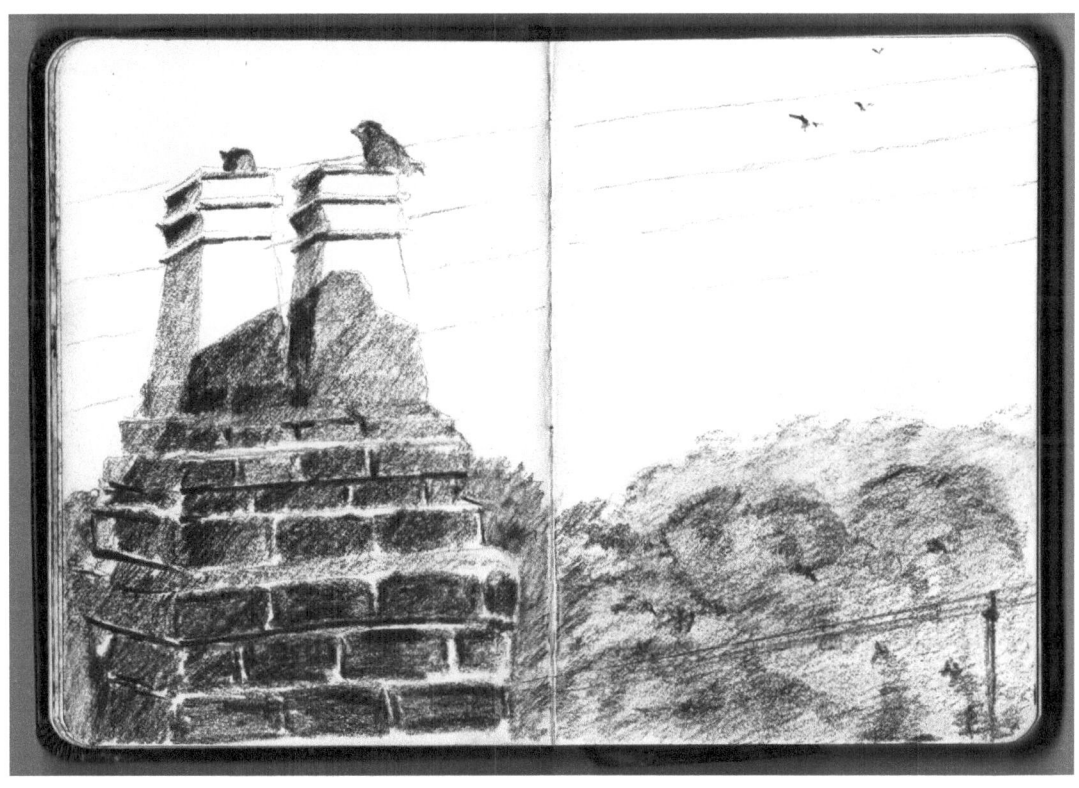

*From my sketchbook 'Observation and Experiment'*

www.ingramcontent.com/pod-product-compliance
Lightning Source LLC
Chambersburg PA
CBHW051054180526
45172CB00002B/627